Post convoction

Lets make law

Chapter 1: Introduction to Post-Conviction Remedies

- Definition of post-conviction remedies
- Importance in the criminal justice system
- Distinguishing appeals from post-conviction petitions
- Overview of the key legal remedies available after conviction

Chapter 2: Appeals and Direct Review

- Overview of the appeals process
- Key differences between appeals and other remedies
- Timeline for filing an appeal
- What can be appealed (legal errors, insufficiency of evidence, etc.)
- Strategies for effective appeals
- Case studies: Successful and unsuccessful appeals

Chapter 3: Habeas Corpus Petitions

- Definition of habeas corpus and its origins
- Federal vs. state habeas corpus procedures
- When and how to file a habeas corpus petition
- Common grounds for habeas relief (constitutional violations, ineffective assistance of counsel, etc.)
- Procedural barriers (exhaustion of state remedies, statute of limitations)
- Significant case law on habeas corpus petitions
- Case study: Landmark habeas corpus cases

Chapter 4: Ineffective Assistance of Counsel

- Defining ineffective assistance of counsel
- The Strickland v. Washington standard

- Proving deficient performance and prejudice
- Filing for post-conviction relief based on ineffective counsel
- Recent developments in case law
- Case study: Winning an ineffective assistance claim

Chapter 5: Newly Discovered Evidence

- Understanding newly discovered evidence claims
- Criteria for filing post-conviction petitions based on new evidence
- Time limits and exceptions for presenting new evidence
- Actual innocence and wrongful convictions
- Case studies: How new evidence changed convictions (e.g., DNA evidence)

Chapter 6: Prosecutorial Misconduct and Judicial Errors

- What constitutes prosecutorial misconduct (withholding evidence, improper arguments)
- Judicial errors during trials and sentencing
- Filing motions for post-conviction relief based on misconduct or judicial error
- Burden of proof and overcoming procedural default
- Case study: High-profile cases of prosecutorial misconduct

Chapter 7: Sentencing Challenges

- Challenging unlawful or excessive sentences
- The role of sentence modification or correction in post-conviction cases
- Retroactive changes in sentencing laws (e.g., the First Step Act)
- Filing for sentence reduction or resentencing

- Case study: Significant sentence reduction victories

Chapter 8: Federal Post-Conviction Remedies: 28 U.S.C. § 2255

- What is a § 2255 motion?
- Differences between § 2255 and habeas corpus under § 2241
- Grounds for § 2255 relief (ineffective counsel, jurisdictional issues, constitutional violations)
- Filing timelines and procedural hurdles
- Case study: Using § 2255 for federal prisoners

Chapter 9: State Post-Conviction Remedies

- State-specific post-conviction laws and procedures
- Differences in remedies between states
- Common state remedies (e.g., state habeas, Rule 3.850 in Florida)
- Collateral attacks on state convictions
- Case study: Successful state post-conviction petitions

Chapter 10: Innocence Projects and Legal Aid for Post-Conviction Relief

- Role of innocence projects and legal aid organizations
- How they assist with post-conviction cases
- Requirements for innocence project representation
- Case study: High-profile exonerations from innocence projects

Chapter 11: Procedural Bars and Timeliness

- Statutes of limitations for post-conviction petitions
- Overcoming procedural defaults
- Equitable tolling and other exceptions to procedural

bars
- Case study: How procedural bars affect post-conviction outcomes

Chapter 12: Strategies for Success

- Key strategies for building a strong post-conviction case
- The role of expert witnesses and forensic evidence
- Collaboration with appellate attorneys and investigators
- Writing an effective post-conviction petition
- Case study: Real-world strategies that led to post-conviction success

Chapter 13: Ethical Considerations in Post-Conviction Representation

- The role of defense attorneys in post-conviction cases
- Navigating the ethical responsibilities of representing convicted individuals
- The importance of zealously advocating for clients even after conviction
- Common ethical dilemmas in post-conviction representation

Chapter 14: The Future of Post-Conviction Remedies

- Recent developments in criminal justice reform
- The impact of changing technology (e.g., DNA testing) on post-conviction cases
- Advocacy for expanding post-conviction rights
- Looking ahead: Potential reforms in state and federal systems

Conclusion: The Path Forward

- Recap of key takeaways from the book
- Encouragement for those seeking post-conviction remedies
- Resources for further reading and legal assistance

This structure provides a comprehensive guide to navigating the complexities of post-conviction remedies. Each chapter could include real-life case studies, practical advice, and legal insights to make the book an indispensable resource for attorneys, inmates, and advocates alike.

Chapter 1: Introduction to Post-Conviction Remedies

The legal system in the United States is designed to provide several layers of protection to individuals accused or convicted of crimes. While the trial process is crucial for determining guilt or innocence, the legal process doesn't end with the jury's verdict or the judge's sentence. Post-conviction remedies are essential for ensuring that justice is served, especially when errors occur during the trial, new evidence emerges, or constitutional rights are violated.

1.1 What are Post-Conviction Remedies?

Post-conviction remedies are legal mechanisms available to convicted individuals to challenge the validity of their conviction or sentence. These remedies are distinct from the direct appeals process, which primarily focuses on errors made during the trial. Post-conviction petitions, on the other hand, often address issues that were not raised or fully resolved on direct appeal.

The key purpose of post-conviction remedies is to correct wrongful convictions, protect constitutional rights, and ensure that justice prevails even after a trial has concluded.

1.2 Importance of Post-Conviction Remedies

Errors in the criminal justice system are not uncommon. From wrongful convictions to sentencing disparities, individuals often face the consequences of mistakes made during investigation, prosecution, or defense. Post-conviction remedies offer an opportunity to correct these errors.

Moreover, they serve as a check on the fairness of the legal system. They provide a path for individuals who have suffered from ineffective assistance of counsel, prosecutorial misconduct, or the emergence of new evidence, such as DNA testing, that could exonerate them.

Post-conviction petitions also play a critical role in ensuring that constitutional violations, such as those involving the Sixth Amendment right to counsel or the Eighth Amendment protection against cruel and unusual punishment, are addressed and remedied.

1.3 Distinguishing Appeals from Post-Conviction Remedies

While both appeals and post-conviction remedies are part of the legal recourse available to convicted individuals, there are significant differences between the two.

- Direct Appeals: After a conviction, the defendant has the right to file a direct appeal. This appeal challenges specific errors that occurred during the trial, such as improperly admitted evidence, incorrect jury instructions, or judicial bias. Appeals focus on the trial record and must be filed within a specific period after the conviction.
- Post-Conviction Petitions: These are often filed after the direct appeal process has been exhausted. Post-conviction petitions can raise issues that were not addressed

during the trial or direct appeal, such as newly discovered evidence, ineffective assistance of counsel, or prosecutorial misconduct. Unlike direct appeals, post-conviction remedies often involve the presentation of new evidence and may require evidentiary hearings.

1.4 Overview of Legal Remedies After Conviction

Post-conviction remedies vary depending on whether the conviction occurred in state or federal court. Generally, the most common forms of post-conviction relief include:

- Habeas Corpus Petitions: A habeas corpus petition challenges the legality of detention, arguing that the defendant is being held in violation of constitutional rights. Both state and federal prisoners can file habeas petitions under certain conditions.
- Motions for a New Trial: These are filed in cases where new evidence emerges that could potentially exonerate the defendant or significantly alter the outcome of the trial.
- Ineffective Assistance of Counsel Claims: Defendants can seek relief if they can demonstrate that their attorney's performance was so deficient that it deprived them of a fair trial.
- Sentence Modifications: In some cases, individuals can challenge their sentence as being unlawful or excessively harsh based on changes in the law or new evidence.

Chapter 2: Appeals and Direct Review

The appeals process is often the first step after a conviction for someone seeking to challenge the outcome of their trial. Unlike post-conviction remedies that focus on errors or evidence arising after a trial, appeals concentrate on mistakes made during the trial itself. Understanding how appeals work is critical for any defendant or attorney aiming to overturn a conviction or reduce a sentence.

2.1 Overview of the Appeals Process

An appeal is a formal request for a higher court to review and reconsider a lower court's decision. The goal is not to re-argue the entire case but to identify legal errors that occurred during the trial and demonstrate how these errors impacted the fairness or outcome of the case.

- Notice of Appeal: The first step in the appeals process is filing a notice of appeal, typically within a short time frame after the conviction (often 30-45 days). This notice informs the court and the opposing party of the intent to challenge the conviction or sentence.
- Appellate Briefs: After the notice is filed, both the defense and the prosecution submit written arguments, known as appellate briefs. The defense argues why the conviction or sentence should be reversed or modified, citing specific legal errors made during the trial. The prosecution responds by defending the trial court's decision and arguing that any errors were harmless and did not affect the outcome.
- Oral Argument: In some cases, the appellate court will hold oral arguments where attorneys for both sides present their case in person and answer the judges' questions. However, many appeals are decided solely on the written briefs.
- Appellate Court Decision: After reviewing the briefs and oral arguments, the appellate court will issue a written decision. The court can affirm the conviction, reverse it, remand the case for a new trial, or modify the sentence.

2.2 Key Differences Between Appeals and Post-Conviction Remedies

It is essential to distinguish appeals from post-conviction

remedies. Appeals are usually limited to reviewing the trial record for legal errors, while post-conviction petitions can introduce new evidence or claims of ineffective assistance of counsel.

- Timing: Appeals must be filed immediately after conviction, usually within a specific timeframe. Post-conviction remedies, on the other hand, can often be pursued after the direct appeal process has been completed.
- Scope: Appeals focus on legal errors made during the trial, such as improper admission of evidence, incorrect jury instructions, or prosecutorial misconduct. Post-conviction petitions can raise issues that go beyond the trial record, such as newly discovered evidence, constitutional violations, or claims of actual innocence.

2.3 Common Grounds for Appeals

To succeed in an appeal, the defense must show that significant legal errors occurred during the trial, and these errors had a material impact on the outcome. Common grounds for appeal include:

- Improper Admission of Evidence: The trial court may have admitted evidence that should have been excluded under the rules of evidence, such as illegally obtained evidence, hearsay, or overly prejudicial material.
- Ineffective Assistance of Counsel: If the defense attorney's performance fell below an acceptable standard and affected the trial's outcome, this can be grounds for an appeal.
- Prosecutorial Misconduct: Appeals can challenge actions by the prosecution, such as withholding exculpatory evidence, making improper arguments, or engaging in unethical behavior during the trial.
- Incorrect Jury Instructions: If the judge gave the jury

incorrect or misleading instructions regarding the law, this could form the basis of an appeal.
- Insufficiency of the Evidence: The defense may argue that the evidence presented at trial was insufficient to support a guilty verdict beyond a reasonable doubt.
- Sentencing Errors: If the trial judge imposed an unlawful or excessively harsh sentence, this could be challenged on appeal.

2.4 Timeline for Filing an Appeal

The timeline for filing an appeal varies by jurisdiction, but it is generally short. Most jurisdictions require that a notice of appeal be filed within 30 to 45 days after the conviction or sentencing. Missing this deadline can bar the defendant from pursuing an appeal, so timing is critical.

Once the notice is filed, the appellate briefs are typically due within a few months. The appeals court may take several months or even years to issue a decision, depending on the complexity of the case and the court's caseload.

2.5 Strategies for Effective Appeals

Winning an appeal requires careful legal strategy and a thorough understanding of the trial record. Some strategies for effective appeals include:

- Identifying Clear Legal Errors: The defense should focus on the most egregious legal errors that occurred during the trial, especially those that had a significant impact on the verdict or sentence.
- Framing Issues Clearly in the Brief: The appellate brief should clearly and persuasively outline the legal issues and provide a concise argument supported by case law.
- Focusing on Constitutional Violations: Appeals based

on constitutional rights violations, such as the right to a fair trial or the right to effective assistance of counsel, tend to receive more scrutiny from appellate courts.
- Effective Use of Case Law: Citing relevant case law that supports the arguments in the appeal is crucial. This demonstrates to the appellate court that similar issues have been resolved in favor of the defendant in other cases.

2.6 Case Studies: Successful and Unsuccessful Appeals

Appeals can succeed or fail based on various factors, including the quality of the legal arguments, the nature of the trial errors, and the composition of the appellate court.

- Successful Appeal Example: In Brady v. Maryland, the U.S. Supreme Court ruled that the prosecution's failure to disclose exculpatory evidence violated the defendant's right to due process. This decision has since become the foundation for appeals based on prosecutorial misconduct involving the withholding of evidence.
- Unsuccessful Appeal Example: In many cases, appellate courts may find that trial errors were "harmless," meaning that even if a mistake was made, it did not significantly impact the verdict or sentencing. In such cases, the conviction may be upheld despite procedural mistakes at trial.

Chapter 3: Habeas Corpus Petitions

Habeas corpus is one of the most critical and historical legal tools for protecting individual liberty in the United States. It provides convicted individuals the opportunity to challenge the legality of their detention. Habeas corpus, often referred to as the "great writ," plays a pivotal role in post-conviction relief at both state and federal levels, providing a lifeline for prisoners who believe their constitutional rights have been violated.

3.1 Understanding Habeas Corpus

The term habeas corpus is Latin for "you shall have the body," which refers to a court order requiring authorities to bring a detained individual before the court to determine whether their detention is lawful. The writ of habeas corpus has a long history in common law, stretching back to the Magna Carta, and is enshrined in the U.S. Constitution.

Habeas corpus petitions are not appeals but rather collateral attacks on the legality of detention, typically focusing on constitutional violations that may have occurred during the trial, sentencing, or other phases of the legal process.

3.2 Federal vs. State Habeas Corpus

Habeas corpus petitions can be filed in both state and federal courts, depending on the nature of the conviction. State prisoners generally file habeas petitions under state law but may turn to federal courts under certain circumstances. Federal prisoners file habeas petitions under federal law, usually through a motion under 28 U.S.C. § 2255.

- State Habeas Corpus: State prisoners who have exhausted their appeals in state court may file a state habeas petition to challenge their conviction or sentence based on constitutional violations or newly discovered evidence. If the state habeas petition is denied, they may then file a federal habeas petition under 28 U.S.C. § 2254.
- Federal Habeas Corpus: Federal prisoners may file a habeas corpus petition under 28 U.S.C. § 2241 or a motion to vacate, set aside, or correct their sentence under 28 U.S.C. § 2255. The § 2255 motion is the primary means for federal prisoners to challenge their conviction or sentence,

particularly if they believe their rights were violated under the U.S. Constitution.

3.3 Grounds for Filing a Habeas Corpus Petition

Habeas corpus petitions are generally based on claims that the prisoner's constitutional rights were violated during their trial, sentencing, or appeal. Common grounds for habeas relief include:

- Ineffective Assistance of Counsel: A claim that the defense attorney's performance was so deficient that it deprived the defendant of a fair trial. The standard for proving ineffective assistance is established in Strickland v. Washington, which requires showing both deficient performance and prejudice.
- Prosecutorial Misconduct: This occurs when the prosecution engages in unlawful or unethical behavior, such as withholding exculpatory evidence (a violation of Brady v. Maryland), making improper arguments, or presenting false evidence.
- Newly Discovered Evidence: Habeas petitions can be based on the discovery of new evidence that was not available during the trial. For example, advances in DNA testing have led to the exoneration of many wrongfully convicted individuals.
- Violation of Constitutional Rights: This can include violations of the right to a fair trial, due process, equal protection, or protection against cruel and unusual punishment (e.g., conditions of confinement that violate the Eighth Amendment).
- Actual Innocence Claims: Some habeas petitions are filed by individuals who claim they are factually innocent of the crime for which they were convicted. These claims typically rely on new evidence or developments that were unavailable during the original trial.

3.4 The Habeas Corpus Process

The process of filing a habeas corpus petition varies slightly between state and federal courts, but the general procedure involves the following steps:

1. Filing the Petition: The first step is to file a written petition for habeas corpus in the appropriate court. The petition must clearly outline the legal and factual grounds for challenging the conviction or sentence.
2. Preliminary Review: The court conducts a preliminary review of the petition to determine whether it presents sufficient grounds to warrant further examination. If the petition is frivolous or does not raise valid claims, the court may dismiss it outright.
3. Answer and Response: If the court decides to consider the petition, the state or federal government (the respondent) is required to file an answer responding to the claims made in the petition. The petitioner may then file a reply to the government's response.
4. Evidentiary Hearing (if necessary): In some cases, the court may hold an evidentiary hearing to consider new evidence or testimony that was not available during the trial. These hearings are relatively rare, but they are sometimes granted in cases involving new evidence, ineffective assistance of counsel, or other significant constitutional violations.
5. Court Decision: After reviewing the petition, the court will issue a decision. If the court grants the writ, it may vacate the conviction, order a new trial, or modify the sentence. If the writ is denied, the petitioner may be able to appeal the decision to a higher court.

3.5 Procedural Barriers to Habeas Corpus Relief

There are several procedural barriers that can make it difficult for prisoners to obtain habeas relief. Some of the most common challenges include:

- Exhaustion of State Remedies: Before a state prisoner can file a federal habeas petition, they must exhaust all available state court remedies. This means they must have presented their constitutional claims to the highest state court before turning to the federal courts.
- Statute of Limitations: The Antiterrorism and Effective Death Penalty Act (AEDPA) imposes a one-year statute of limitations on filing a federal habeas petition. The one-year period begins when the conviction becomes final or when new evidence is discovered, depending on the nature of the claim.
- Procedural Default: If a prisoner fails to raise a constitutional claim during the trial or on direct appeal, they may be barred from raising it in a habeas petition. Procedural default can be overcome in certain cases, such as when the failure to raise the issue was due to ineffective assistance of counsel.
- Successive Petitions: Federal courts generally do not allow prisoners to file multiple habeas petitions raising the same claims. Successive petitions are only permitted in limited circumstances, such as when new evidence is discovered or when a new legal rule is announced by the Supreme Court.

3.6 Landmark Habeas Corpus Cases

Several landmark cases have shaped the development of habeas corpus law in the United States. These cases demonstrate the significance of the writ in protecting individual rights and correcting wrongful convictions:

- Gideon v. Wainwright (1963): This case established

the right to counsel for indigent defendants in criminal cases. Clarence Gideon filed a habeas corpus petition after being denied a lawyer at his trial, and the Supreme Court ruled that the Sixth Amendment guarantees the right to counsel in all felony cases.
- Brady v. Maryland (1963): In this case, the Supreme Court held that the prosecution's failure to disclose exculpatory evidence violated the defendant's due process rights. This case has become the foundation for habeas petitions based on prosecutorial misconduct.
- Strickland v. Washington (1984): This case established the standard for evaluating claims of ineffective assistance of counsel. The Court held that to succeed on an ineffective assistance claim, the defendant must show both that the attorney's performance was deficient and that the deficient performance prejudiced the defense.

Here is a basic example of a Habeas Corpus Petition Form that can be adapted for filing in either state or federal court, depending on the jurisdiction. This form is generic and should be customized according to the specific rules of the court in which the petition will be filed.

United States District Court

___ (Insert the name of the appropriate District Court) ___
For the ___ (Insert District) ___

Petitioner:
___ (Full Name of Petitioner) ___
___ (Prison Identification Number) ___
___ (Name of Institution) ___
___ (Mailing Address of Prison) ___

Respondent:
___ (Name of Warden, Superintendent, or other custodian)

___ (Name of Institution) ___
___ (Institution Address) ___

Case No.:
___ (To be filled in by the Court) ___

PETITION FOR WRIT OF HABEAS CORPUS

Pursuant to 28 U.S.C. § 2254 (for state prisoners) or 28 U.S.C. § 2255 (for federal prisoners)

1. Name and location of court where judgment of conviction was entered:

___ (e.g., Superior Court of ___ County, State of ___, or United States District Court for the ___ District) ___

2. Date of judgment of conviction:

___ (Month, Day, Year) ___

3. Length of sentence:

___ (Insert the length of the sentence imposed) ___

4. Nature of offense(s) for which you were convicted:

___ (List all offenses for which you were convicted and sentenced) ___

5. Are you currently serving this sentence?

___ Yes ___ No (If "No," provide details) ___

6. Have you filed an appeal or any other post-conviction

petitions challenging this conviction?

___ Yes ___ No (If "Yes," provide details, including the courts and dates of the filings, and the outcome.) ___

7. Grounds for Habeas Corpus Petition:

State each ground on which you are seeking habeas corpus relief, and provide supporting facts for each ground. You may attach additional pages if needed.

Ground One:
___ (State the legal ground, such as ineffective assistance of counsel, newly discovered evidence, or prosecutorial misconduct) ___

Supporting Facts:
___ (Provide the specific facts supporting your claim for relief) ___

Ground Two:
___ (State the legal ground) ___

Supporting Facts:
___ (Provide supporting facts) ___

Ground Three:
___ (State the legal ground) ___

Supporting Facts:
___ (Provide supporting facts) ___

8. Relief Requested:

Explain what relief you are requesting from the court (e.g., vacating the conviction, ordering a new trial, or modifying the sentence).

___ (State the relief you are seeking) ___

9. Exhaustion of Remedies:

Have you exhausted all available state or federal remedies, including appeals and state post-conviction petitions?
___ Yes ___ No (If "No," explain why) ___

10. Timeliness of Petition:

Explain why this petition is being filed within the statute of limitations or why there should be an exception to the statute of limitations. (For federal petitions under § 2254 or § 2255, the Antiterrorism and Effective Death Penalty Act imposes a one-year deadline for filing.)

___ (Explain timeliness) ___

DECLARATION UNDER PENALTY OF PERJURY

I declare under penalty of perjury that the foregoing is true and correct to the best of my knowledge and belief.

Executed on ___ (Date) ___

(Signature of Petitioner)
___ (Printed Name) ___

CERTIFICATE OF SERVICE

I hereby certify that a copy of this petition has been mailed to the appropriate court and served on the respondent.

___ (Date) ___

(Signature of Petitioner)

This form provides the basic structure for a habeas corpus petition. Ensure that it is filled out with accurate and complete information, and it may need to be adjusted depending on state-specific or federal-specific procedures. For example, some courts may require the inclusion of a "Memorandum of Law" supporting the legal arguments in the petition.
Below is a template for a Notice of Appeal. This document serves as the official notification to the court and the opposing party that the petitioner intends to appeal a decision made by a lower court.

United States District Court

___ (Insert District) ___

Petitioner/Appellant:
___ (Full Name of Petitioner) ___
___ (Prison Identification Number) ___
___ (Name of Institution) ___
___ (Mailing Address) ___

Respondent/Appellee:
___ (Name of Warden, Superintendent, or other custodian) ___
___ (Name of Institution) ___
___ (Institution Address) ___

Case No.:
___ (Original case number from the lower court) ___

NOTICE OF APPEAL

Notice is hereby given that ___ (Full Name of Petitioner/

Appellant) ___, the petitioner in the above-named case, hereby appeals to the ___ (Insert name of appellate court, such as the United States Court of Appeals for the ___ Circuit) ___ from the judgment entered in this action on ___ (Insert date of judgment or order) ___ by the ___ (Insert name of lower court, such as the United States District Court for the ___ District or State Court name) ___.

The appellant appeals the following decision(s):
___ (Briefly describe the decision being appealed, e.g., "denial of habeas corpus petition," "conviction on counts ___ and sentence") ___.

Grounds for Appeal (optional):

The appellant asserts that the following errors occurred during the proceedings and form the basis for this appeal:
___ (List and briefly describe the legal errors or grounds for appeal, if you choose to include them in the notice. This is not required, but some jurisdictions allow it.) ___

Relief Requested on Appeal:

The appellant respectfully requests that the appellate court reverse the decision of the lower court and grant the relief sought in the original petition/complaint, or in the alternative, order a new trial or resentencing.

Signature and Date:

___ (Date) ___

___ (Signature of Appellant or Attorney) ___
___ (Printed Name of Appellant or Attorney) ___

Certificate of Service:

I hereby certify that a copy of this Notice of Appeal was served on the respondent(s) by mail on ____ (Date) ____ at the following address:
____ (Name and Address of Respondent's Counsel or the opposing party, usually the prosecuting attorney) ____

(Signature of Appellant or Attorney)
____ (Printed Name) ____

Instructions for Filing:

- The Notice of Appeal must be filed with the clerk of the court where the original judgment was entered.
- Depending on the jurisdiction, there may be a filing fee associated with the notice. If the appellant is unable to pay the fee, a request for waiver may be submitted.
- Ensure that the notice is filed within the time limits for appeals, which are often 30 days from the date of the judgment or order being appealed.

This form serves as the official notice that the petitioner/appellant is initiating an appeal. It should be filled out with the proper case information and filed with the appropriate court within the prescribed time limits.

Chapter 4: Ineffective Assistance of Counsel

Ineffective assistance of counsel is one of the most frequently raised grounds in post-conviction petitions. The Sixth Amendment of the U.S. Constitution guarantees the right to counsel, but this right is not fulfilled simply by the presence of an attorney. The attorney's performance must meet a minimum standard of competence. When this standard is not met, and the defendant is prejudiced as a result, the courts may grant relief, including vacating a conviction or ordering a new trial.

4.1 Defining Ineffective Assistance of Counsel

To claim ineffective assistance of counsel, a defendant must demonstrate that their attorney's representation was not only below an objective standard of reasonableness but also that this inadequate representation affected the outcome of the case. The legal standard for ineffective assistance was established in the U.S. Supreme Court case Strickland v. Washington.

The Strickland standard involves a two-part test:

- Deficient Performance: The petitioner must show that their attorney's performance fell below an objective standard of reasonableness. The court looks at whether the attorney's actions were so far outside the range of professionally competent assistance that they violated the defendant's right to counsel.
- Prejudice: The petitioner must also demonstrate that there is a reasonable probability that, but for the attorney's unprofessional errors, the result of the proceeding would have been different. A reasonable probability is one sufficient to undermine confidence in the outcome.

4.2 Examples of Ineffective Assistance

There are many ways in which an attorney's performance can be considered ineffective. Some common examples include:

- Failure to Investigate: A defense attorney is obligated to thoroughly investigate the facts of the case, interview witnesses, and seek out exculpatory evidence. A failure to do so can be grounds for an ineffective assistance claim.
- Failure to Present a Defense: If an attorney fails to present a valid defense, such as an alibi or evidence of self-

defense, the defendant may have a claim for ineffective assistance.
- **Failure to Object to Improper Evidence:** If a defense attorney fails to object to the introduction of inadmissible evidence, such as hearsay or evidence obtained in violation of the Fourth Amendment, this may constitute ineffective assistance.
- **Failure to File Appropriate Motions:** A defense attorney is expected to file necessary pre-trial and trial motions, including motions to suppress illegally obtained evidence, dismiss charges, or challenge jury instructions. Failing to do so can lead to an ineffective assistance claim.
- **Failure to Communicate Plea Offers:** Defense attorneys must inform their clients of all plea offers made by the prosecution. If an attorney fails to communicate a plea deal that could have led to a lesser sentence or alternative resolution, this may be grounds for a claim.
- **Conflicts of Interest:** An attorney representing multiple clients with conflicting interests may provide ineffective assistance if the conflict affects their ability to advocate zealously on behalf of one client.

4.3 The Strickland Test: Proving Deficient Performance

The first prong of the Strickland test requires the petitioner to prove that their attorney's performance was deficient. Courts are generally deferential to attorneys' professional judgments, and it is not enough to show that a different attorney might have chosen a different strategy. The petitioner must show that the attorney's actions were objectively unreasonable under the circumstances.

Some factors the courts consider when evaluating deficient performance include:

- The complexity of the case and the attorney's

familiarity with the applicable law
- Whether the attorney made informed decisions after adequate investigation
- Whether the attorney's trial strategy was sound, even if it ultimately failed
- Whether the attorney's actions deviated from accepted professional norms

4.4 Proving Prejudice: The Impact on the Outcome

The second prong of the Strickland test requires the petitioner to demonstrate prejudice. This means showing that, but for the attorney's errors, there is a reasonable probability that the outcome of the trial or sentencing would have been different.

This is often the more difficult part of the test to meet. Even if the attorney's performance was clearly deficient, courts may still deny the claim if the evidence against the defendant was overwhelming or if it seems unlikely that the attorney's errors materially affected the outcome.

For example:

- If an attorney fails to file a motion to suppress evidence, the petitioner must show that the evidence would have been suppressed and that this suppression would have affected the outcome of the trial.
- If an attorney fails to present a key witness, the petitioner must demonstrate that the witness's testimony would have been favorable and likely to change the jury's verdict.

4.5 Case Law on Ineffective Assistance of Counsel

Numerous cases have helped define the boundaries of what constitutes ineffective assistance of counsel. Some landmark decisions include:

- **Strickland v. Washington (1984)**: This case established the two-part test for determining whether counsel was ineffective. In Strickland, the Supreme Court found that, while the attorney's performance may have been substandard, it did not prejudice the defendant to the extent required for a new trial.
- **Lafler v. Cooper (2012)**: In this case, the Supreme Court held that a defendant could claim ineffective assistance if their attorney's bad advice led them to reject a plea bargain and go to trial, where they received a harsher sentence.
- **Rompilla v. Beard (2005)**: In this case, the Supreme Court found that defense counsel's failure to review the defendant's prior conviction records and use them in mitigating evidence for sentencing amounted to ineffective assistance.

4.6 Filing a Post-Conviction Petition Based on Ineffective Assistance

A claim of ineffective assistance of counsel can be raised in a direct appeal, but it is often pursued through post-conviction relief petitions, such as a habeas corpus petition. In many cases, these claims are first raised in state court before being brought to federal court.

The process for filing a petition based on ineffective assistance generally involves:

1. **Gathering Evidence**: The petitioner must provide evidence showing how their attorney's performance was deficient. This might include affidavits from witnesses, legal filings, or expert testimony about the attorney's performance.
2. **Filing the Petition**: The petitioner files a petition for post-conviction relief or a habeas corpus petition in state or

federal court. The petition must outline the specific ways in which the attorney's performance was deficient and how this impacted the outcome.

3. Evidentiary Hearing: In some cases, the court may hold an evidentiary hearing to hear from witnesses and review new evidence that was not presented at trial.

4. Court's Decision: The court will determine whether the petitioner has met both prongs of the Strickland test. If the court finds in favor of the petitioner, it may order a new trial, vacate the conviction, or modify the sentence.

4.7 Case Study: A Successful Ineffective Assistance Claim

In Lafler v. Cooper, the defendant rejected a plea bargain based on his attorney's incorrect advice that he could not be convicted of the charges he faced at trial. The defendant subsequently went to trial, where he was convicted and received a sentence much harsher than the plea offer. The Supreme Court ruled that the attorney's bad advice constituted ineffective assistance, and the case was remanded for a new sentencing hearing.

Chapter 5: Newly Discovered Evidence

Newly discovered evidence can be a powerful basis for post-conviction relief. Often, this evidence emerges long after a trial has concluded, and it may reveal information that was not available during the original proceedings. This type of evidence can range from physical evidence, such as DNA, to witness testimony that was previously unavailable or suppressed. When such evidence has the potential to prove innocence or significantly alter the outcome of a trial, courts may grant relief in the form of a new trial, the dismissal of charges, or the modification of a sentence.

5.1 Defining Newly Discovered Evidence

Newly discovered evidence is any relevant and material evidence that could not have been discovered with reasonable diligence before or during the trial. This evidence may be completely new or may involve an alternative interpretation of existing evidence, such as scientific advancements (e.g., DNA testing) that were not available at the time of the original trial.

The petitioner must demonstrate that the newly discovered evidence is not merely cumulative or impeaching but instead would have likely changed the outcome of the trial. The court's focus is on whether the evidence could create reasonable doubt about the defendant's guilt.

5.2 Types of Newly Discovered Evidence

There are several types of newly discovered evidence that can form the basis for post-conviction relief. Some of the most common include:

- DNA and Forensic Testing: Technological advances in forensic science, such as DNA testing, have led to the exoneration of many wrongfully convicted individuals. For example, if biological evidence from a crime scene can be tested for DNA that excludes the defendant as the perpetrator, this can serve as powerful newly discovered evidence.
- Witness Recantations: In some cases, a key witness from the original trial may recant their testimony, admitting that they lied under oath or were coerced into testifying falsely. A witness recantation can undermine the integrity of the original conviction, especially if the witness's testimony was central to the prosecution's case.
- Suppressed or Withheld Evidence: Sometimes, the prosecution fails to disclose exculpatory evidence, violating the defendant's constitutional rights under Brady v. Maryland.

If such evidence comes to light after the trial, it can be the basis for a newly discovered evidence claim. This could include police reports, forensic findings, or witness statements that were improperly withheld from the defense.
- New Witnesses or Testimony: If new witnesses emerge who were not available during the original trial, and their testimony supports the defendant's innocence or contradicts the prosecution's case, this can be grounds for relief. For example, a previously unknown eyewitness who can provide an alibi for the defendant might meet the criteria for newly discovered evidence.
- Expert Testimony: In some cases, expert testimony that was not available during the original trial may qualify as newly discovered evidence. For example, if new scientific techniques disprove the validity of forensic evidence used at trial, expert testimony challenging that evidence could warrant a new trial.

5.3 Criteria for Post-Conviction Relief Based on Newly Discovered Evidence

Courts apply strict criteria when evaluating post-conviction petitions based on newly discovered evidence. The petitioner typically must meet the following standards:

1. The Evidence Could Not Have Been Discovered with Due Diligence: The petitioner must show that the newly discovered evidence was not known at the time of the trial and could not have been discovered with reasonable diligence. This prevents defendants from using evidence that was available but overlooked during the trial.
2. The Evidence is Material to the Case: The newly discovered evidence must be directly related to the defendant's guilt or innocence, or to an essential element of the crime. It cannot be merely tangential or irrelevant to the issues in the case.

3. The Evidence is Not Merely Impeaching or Cumulative: Courts generally do not grant relief if the newly discovered evidence is simply for impeaching a witness's credibility or repeating evidence that was already presented at trial. The evidence must offer new, substantive information that was not previously available.

4. The Evidence Would Likely Have Changed the Outcome of the Trial: The petitioner must demonstrate that the newly discovered evidence is of such significance that it would have likely led to a different result at trial. This is often the most difficult standard to meet, as courts are reluctant to overturn convictions unless the new evidence casts serious doubt on the original verdict.

5.4 Filing a Motion for a New Trial Based on Newly Discovered Evidence

A motion for a new trial based on newly discovered evidence is typically filed in the trial court where the original conviction occurred. The procedure for filing such a motion varies by jurisdiction, but the general process involves the following steps:

1. Drafting the Motion: The petitioner (or their attorney) drafts a motion for a new trial that explains the nature of the newly discovered evidence, why it was not available during the trial, and how it meets the criteria for granting relief.

2. Supporting Documentation: The motion must include affidavits, reports, or other documentation supporting the claim of newly discovered evidence. For example, if the new evidence is DNA test results, the petitioner should include the laboratory reports and expert affidavits explaining the significance of the results.

3. Filing the Motion: The motion is filed with the trial court along with a request for a hearing. Some courts require that the motion be filed within a specific timeframe after the

discovery of the new evidence, so it is important to act quickly.

4. Evidentiary Hearing: If the court grants a hearing, both parties will have the opportunity to present evidence and argue their case. The petitioner will need to demonstrate that the newly discovered evidence meets the legal standards for relief, while the prosecution will likely argue that the evidence does not warrant overturning the conviction.

5. Court's Decision: After the hearing, the court will issue a ruling. If the court finds that the newly discovered evidence is sufficient to undermine the conviction, it may grant a new trial, modify the sentence, or even dismiss the charges.

5.5 Timeliness and Statute of Limitations

Many jurisdictions impose strict time limits for filing motions based on newly discovered evidence. The clock typically begins to run when the evidence is discovered or could have been discovered with reasonable diligence. In federal cases, the Antiterrorism and Effective Death Penalty Act (AEDPA) imposes a one-year statute of limitations on filing habeas corpus petitions, but exceptions may apply if the newly discovered evidence could not have been found earlier.

It is essential to act swiftly once new evidence is discovered to avoid missing critical deadlines. In some cases, the court may grant an extension or allow a late filing if there is a valid reason for the delay, but these exceptions are rare and must be supported by compelling circumstances.

5.6 Case Studies: Successful Claims of Newly Discovered Evidence

Several notable cases have resulted in exonerations or new trials based on newly discovered evidence. Here are a few examples:

- The Case of Kirk Bloodsworth (1993): Kirk Bloodsworth was the first person in the U.S. to be exonerated from death row based on DNA evidence. Bloodsworth had been convicted of the rape and murder of a nine-year-old girl in Maryland, but new DNA testing proved that he was not the perpetrator. After spending nearly nine years in prison, Bloodsworth was released, and his case became a landmark in the use of DNA evidence in criminal justice.
- The Central Park Five (2002): The Central Park Five were five teenagers wrongfully convicted of assaulting a jogger in Central Park, New York, in 1989. They spent years in prison before new DNA evidence and a confession from the actual perpetrator exonerated them in 2002. The newly discovered evidence proved that none of the five teenagers were involved in the crime, and their convictions were vacated.

5.7 DNA Testing and the Evolution of Forensic Science

One of the most significant developments in the area of newly discovered evidence is the advent of DNA testing and advancements in forensic science. DNA testing has revolutionized post-conviction litigation, providing a scientific basis for proving innocence in many cases where physical evidence was previously unavailable or unreliable.

In addition to DNA testing, other forensic advancements, such as fingerprint analysis, ballistics testing, and digital forensics, have also contributed to the discovery of new evidence that can challenge wrongful convictions.

Chapter 6: Prosecutorial Misconduct and Judicial Errors

Prosecutorial misconduct and judicial errors are significant grounds for post-conviction relief. Both can severely undermine the fairness of a trial and result in wrongful convictions or unjust sentences. While prosecutors are sworn to uphold justice, misconduct such as withholding evidence or improper arguments can compromise a defendant's right to a fair trial. Similarly, judicial errors, including improper rulings or failure to instruct the jury correctly, can significantly impact the outcome of a case.

6.1 Prosecutorial Misconduct

Prosecutorial misconduct occurs when a prosecutor engages in behavior that violates legal or ethical standards, leading to an unfair trial. Prosecutors have immense power in the courtroom, and when they abuse that power, the consequences can be devastating for defendants.

Types of Prosecutorial Misconduct:

- Withholding Exculpatory Evidence (Brady Violations): In Brady v. Maryland (1963), the U.S. Supreme Court held that prosecutors are required to disclose any evidence that is favorable to the defense and material to guilt or punishment. Failure to disclose such evidence is known as a "Brady violation" and can result in the overturning of a conviction if the withheld evidence could have changed the outcome of the trial.
- False Evidence or Testimony: If a prosecutor knowingly presents false evidence or allows a witness to give false testimony, it constitutes misconduct. The U.S. Supreme Court has ruled that convictions obtained through the use of false evidence violate the defendant's due process rights.
- Improper Arguments: During closing arguments, prosecutors may engage in misconduct by making inflammatory remarks, vouching for the credibility of witnesses, or suggesting facts not in evidence. These tactics can unfairly sway the jury and undermine the defendant's right to an impartial trial.

- Improper Cross-Examination: Prosecutors sometimes engage in improper questioning during cross-examination, such as badgering a witness, asking irrelevant or inflammatory questions, or introducing inadmissible evidence.
- Selective Prosecution: Prosecutorial misconduct can also occur when prosecutors unfairly target individuals for prosecution based on their race, religion, or other discriminatory factors. If selective prosecution can be proven, it may be grounds for relief.

Case Law on Prosecutorial Misconduct:

- Brady v. Maryland (1963): This landmark case established that suppression of exculpatory evidence by the prosecution violates the defendant's due process rights. Brady violations are one of the most common forms of prosecutorial misconduct cited in post-conviction petitions.
- Napue v. Illinois (1959): The U.S. Supreme Court held that a conviction obtained through the use of false testimony known to be false by the prosecution violates due process, even if the false testimony pertains only to the credibility of a witness.

6.2 Judicial Errors

Judicial errors occur when a judge makes incorrect rulings during the trial that negatively impact the fairness of the proceedings. While not every mistake by a judge is considered grounds for post-conviction relief, certain types of errors can be significant enough to warrant a new trial or a modification of the sentence.

Types of Judicial Errors:

- Incorrect Jury Instructions: Jury instructions are the directions a judge gives to the jury regarding the laws that apply to the case. If a judge gives incorrect or misleading instructions, it can cause the jury to misunderstand the law and apply it incorrectly. This is a common ground for appeal or post-conviction relief.

- Evidentiary Rulings: Judges are responsible for determining which evidence is admissible at trial. If a judge improperly excludes critical defense evidence or allows the jury to hear inadmissible, prejudicial evidence, this can be a judicial error that affects the trial's outcome.
- Improper Sentencing: A judge must follow the law when imposing a sentence. If a judge imposes a sentence that exceeds the statutory maximum or fails to consider mandatory sentencing guidelines, it can be grounds for post-conviction relief.
- Bias or Improper Conduct: Judicial bias or misconduct occurs when a judge demonstrates favoritism toward one side or acts inappropriately during the trial. This could include making biased remarks, prejudging the case, or engaging in ex parte communications (discussions with one party without the other present).

Case Law on Judicial Errors:

- Henderson v. Kibbe (1977): In this case, the U.S. Supreme Court ruled that improper jury instructions can be grounds for reversal if the instructions likely misled the jury in a way that prejudiced the defendant.
- Chapman v. California (1967): The Court held that not all judicial errors require automatic reversal of a conviction. The error must have affected the defendant's substantial rights. However, some constitutional errors, such as bias, are considered "structural errors" and automatically result in reversal.

6.3 Filing for Post-Conviction Relief Based on Prosecutorial Misconduct or Judicial Errors

Defendants who believe their conviction was affected by prosecutorial misconduct or judicial errors can seek post-conviction relief through a variety of legal mechanisms. The specific approach depends on the nature of the error and whether it was raised during the trial or direct appeal.

Steps to File a Post-Conviction Petition:

1. Identify the Misconduct or Error: The first step is to identify the specific instance(s) of prosecutorial misconduct or judicial error that occurred during the trial or sentencing. This requires reviewing the trial transcript, motions, and evidence to find any improper behavior or rulings.
2. Gather Supporting Evidence: Prosecutorial misconduct claims often rely on newly discovered evidence, such as previously withheld exculpatory material. Judicial errors typically involve a review of the court record and legal arguments showing how the judge's rulings deviated from accepted legal standards.
3. File a Motion for Post-Conviction Relief: The defendant or their attorney files a post-conviction petition or motion with the trial court or a higher court. The petition must outline the misconduct or errors and explain how they impacted the outcome of the case.
4. Request an Evidentiary Hearing: In many cases, the defendant may request an evidentiary hearing to present new evidence or call witnesses. The court will then decide whether the misconduct or error was serious enough to justify a new trial, dismissal of charges, or modification of the sentence.
5. Appeal if Necessary: If the post-conviction petition is denied, the defendant may have the right to appeal that decision to a higher court.

6.4 Burden of Proof in Post-Conviction Claims

In post-conviction proceedings, the burden of proof lies with the petitioner. The petitioner must show that the prosecutorial misconduct or judicial error was not only present but also prejudiced the outcome of the trial. In cases involving prosecutorial misconduct, it is necessary to prove that the misconduct was "material," meaning it had a significant impact on the jury's decision.

For judicial errors, the petitioner must demonstrate that the error was not "harmless." Courts apply the "harmless error" doctrine, which allows convictions to stand if the error did not substantially affect the verdict. However, some errors, such as violations of constitutional rights, may be considered "structural errors" that automatically require reversal.

6.5 Remedies for Prosecutorial Misconduct and Judicial Errors

When a court finds that prosecutorial misconduct or judicial errors tainted the original trial, several remedies may be available:

- **New Trial:** The most common remedy is an order for a new trial, especially if the misconduct or error affected the fairness of the original trial.
- **Dismissal of Charges:** In cases of egregious misconduct, such as the intentional suppression of exculpatory evidence, courts may dismiss the charges entirely.
- **Modification of Sentence:** If the misconduct or error occurred during sentencing, the court may order a resentencing hearing to correct the mistake.

6.6 Case Study: Prosecutorial Misconduct in the Duke Lacrosse Case

The Duke Lacrosse case is a well-known example of prosecutorial misconduct. In 2006, several members of the Duke University lacrosse team were accused of sexual assault. The district attorney, Mike Nifong, withheld exculpatory DNA evidence that would have exonerated the defendants. Nifong also made inflammatory public statements about the case, violating the defendants' right to a fair trial. The misconduct was eventually uncovered, and the charges were dropped. Nifong was disbarred for his unethical conduct, and the defendants were fully exonerated.

6.7 Case Study: Judicial Error in the Sam Sheppard Case

The case of Dr. Sam Sheppard, a physician convicted of murdering his wife in 1954, highlights the impact of judicial error on the fairness of a trial. The trial judge in Sheppard's case failed to control the media coverage, resulting in a "circus-like" atmosphere that violated Sheppard's right to a fair trial. The U.S. Supreme Court eventually overturned his conviction in Sheppard v. Maxwell (1966), citing the judge's failure to protect the defendant from the prejudicial effects of pervasive and inflammatory media coverage.

Chapter 7: Sentencing Challenges

After a conviction, sentencing becomes a crucial phase where the court imposes a penalty based on the crime committed. While most sentences are determined by statutes and sentencing guidelines, errors can occur in this process. Additionally, changes in the law, new evidence, or evolving circumstances may allow for post-conviction challenges to sentences. Sentencing challenges are an important aspect of post-conviction relief, as they offer an opportunity to reduce or modify an unjust or excessive sentence.

7.1 Grounds for Challenging a Sentence

There are several grounds on which a defendant can challenge a sentence after conviction. These challenges may be based on legal errors, constitutional violations, or changes in sentencing law. Common grounds include:

- Illegal Sentences: If a court imposes a sentence that is not authorized by law, such as exceeding the statutory maximum or failing to follow mandatory minimums, the sentence may be challenged as illegal. An illegal sentence can be corrected at any time.
- Excessive Sentences: Even if a sentence is technically within the legal range, it may still be challenged if it is deemed disproportionate to the offense. Excessive sentencing claims are often based on the Eighth Amendment, which prohibits cruel and unusual punishment.
- Sentencing Errors: A defendant may challenge a sentence based on procedural errors that occurred during the sentencing phase. For example, if the judge relied on incorrect or incomplete information when determining the sentence, this could form the basis of a post-conviction challenge.
- Ineffective Assistance of Counsel: Ineffective assistance of counsel can also occur during sentencing. If a defense attorney failed to present mitigating evidence or failed to challenge improper sentencing guidelines, the defendant may be able to seek post-conviction relief on this basis.
- Changes in Law: Sentencing laws evolve over time. In some cases, new laws may apply retroactively, allowing individuals who were sentenced under older, harsher guidelines to seek sentence reductions. For example, the First Step Act of 2018 allowed for retroactive reductions in sentences for certain drug offenses under the Fair Sentencing Act of 2010.
- Post-Conviction Rehabilitation: Some jurisdictions

allow defendants to seek sentence reductions based on evidence of rehabilitation while incarcerated. If a defendant can demonstrate that they have made significant efforts to reform, the court may consider modifying their sentence.

7.2 Filing a Motion to Correct or Reduce a Sentence

To challenge a sentence, a defendant typically files a motion with the court that imposed the original sentence. The specific type of motion depends on the grounds for the challenge. Common post-conviction motions related to sentencing include:

- Motion to Correct an Illegal Sentence: This motion is used when the defendant believes their sentence exceeds the legal maximum, violates sentencing guidelines, or is otherwise unauthorized by law.
- Motion for Sentence Reduction: In cases where a change in the law allows for retroactive sentence reductions, the defendant may file a motion for sentence reduction. These motions are often filed under statutes like 18 U.S.C. § 3582(c) for federal prisoners or equivalent state statutes.
- Motion for Resentencing Based on New Evidence: If new evidence emerges that could affect the sentence, such as newly discovered mitigating factors or evidence of actual innocence, the defendant may seek resentencing based on this new information.
- Motion for Compassionate Release: Compassionate release motions are typically based on medical or humanitarian grounds, such as terminal illness or extraordinary family circumstances. These motions are often filed under 18 U.S.C. § 3582(c)(1)(A) in federal cases.

7.3 Sentencing Guidelines and Mandatory Minimums

Sentencing guidelines play a significant role in determining the length and severity of sentences for federal and state crimes. Federal courts use the United States Sentencing Guidelines, which provide a framework for sentencing based on the severity of the crime and the defendant's criminal history. However, these guidelines are advisory rather than mandatory.

- Sentencing Guidelines: Judges use these guidelines to calculate the sentencing range for a particular offense. While judges have some discretion to deviate from the guidelines, significant departures must be justified in the record.
- Mandatory Minimums: Some crimes, particularly drug offenses and violent crimes, carry mandatory minimum sentences that judges must impose regardless of mitigating circumstances. Mandatory minimums are a frequent target of sentencing reform efforts, as they often result in disproportionately harsh sentences.

7.4 Challenging Sentences Under New Laws

Changes in the law can provide defendants with an opportunity to seek sentence reductions or modifications. This is particularly true when new legislation applies retroactively to individuals who were sentenced under outdated or harsher guidelines.

- The First Step Act: One of the most significant pieces of sentencing reform legislation in recent years is the First Step Act of 2018. This federal law allows for retroactive reductions in sentences for certain non-violent drug offenders who were sentenced under the pre-2010 crack cocaine sentencing guidelines. The Act also expanded the availability of compassionate release and gave judges more discretion in sentencing decisions.
- Retroactive Sentencing Guidelines: In some cases,

the U.S. Sentencing Commission or state legislatures may amend sentencing guidelines and make these changes retroactive. Defendants who were sentenced under the old guidelines may file motions to have their sentences reduced under the new rules.

7.5 Eighth Amendment and Excessive Sentences

The Eighth Amendment to the U.S. Constitution prohibits the imposition of "cruel and unusual punishment." This protection extends to sentencing, where it can be used to challenge sentences that are grossly disproportionate to the crime committed.

Proportionality Principle:

- The U.S. Supreme Court has recognized the "proportionality principle" in sentencing, which requires that the severity of a sentence be proportional to the offense. However, courts have generally given wide latitude to legislatures in setting sentencing ranges, and successful proportionality challenges are rare.
- Case Law: In Solem v. Helm (1983), the Supreme Court struck down a life sentence without parole for a non-violent repeat offender, ruling that the sentence was disproportionate to the crime. In contrast, in Harmelin v. Michigan (1991), the Court upheld a mandatory life sentence without parole for a first-time drug offender, emphasizing that only extreme cases of disproportionate sentencing would violate the Eighth Amendment.

7.6 Ineffective Assistance of Counsel During Sentencing

Ineffective assistance of counsel can occur not only during the trial but also during sentencing. Defense attorneys have an obligation to advocate for the most favorable sentence possible and to present mitigating evidence that may lead to a reduced sentence.

Examples of Ineffective Assistance During Sentencing:

- Failure to Present Mitigating Evidence: If the defense attorney fails to present evidence that could result in a lighter sentence, such as the defendant's mental health history, family circumstances, or post-offense rehabilitation efforts, this may be grounds for a sentencing challenge.
- Failure to Object to Sentencing Errors: Defense attorneys must ensure that the court follows proper procedures during sentencing. Failure to object to errors, such as incorrect calculations under the sentencing guidelines or improper consideration of aggravating factors, can lead to an ineffective assistance claim.

7.7 Compassionate Release and Sentence Modifications

In certain circumstances, defendants may seek sentence modifications based on medical or humanitarian reasons. Compassionate release allows prisoners to be released early due to terminal illness, advanced age, or other extraordinary circumstances. These requests are typically evaluated based on:

- Medical Condition: A prisoner suffering from a terminal illness or debilitating medical condition that significantly reduces their ability to function in a correctional facility may be eligible for compassionate release.
- Family Circumstances: In some cases, a prisoner may seek compassionate release due to the death or incapacitation of a primary caregiver for their children or other extraordinary family circumstances.

Federal compassionate release motions are governed by 18

U.S.C. § 3582(c)(1)(A). Recent changes under the First Step Act allow prisoners to file these motions directly with the court, rather than waiting for the Bureau of Prisons to file on their behalf.

7.8 Case Studies: Successful Sentencing Challenges

- The Case of Weldon Angelos: Weldon Angelos was sentenced to 55 years in federal prison for selling small amounts of marijuana while possessing a firearm. His sentence was widely criticized as disproportionate, and after years of advocacy and legal challenges, he was granted clemency by President Barack Obama in 2016. The First Step Act later provided mechanisms for individuals like Angelos to seek reductions in mandatory minimum sentences.
- Compassionate Release During COVID-19: The COVID-19 pandemic led to a significant increase in compassionate release motions, particularly for prisoners with underlying medical conditions. Courts granted compassionate release to many prisoners whose age and health put them at high risk of severe illness from the virus.

This chapter highlights the avenues available for challenging or modifying sentences post-conviction. Whether based on legal errors, changes in the law, or humanitarian reasons, these challenges provide hope for individuals facing unjust or excessive sentences.

Chapter 8: Federal Post-Conviction Remedies: 28 U.S.C. § 2255

Federal prisoners have a specific legal mechanism to challenge their convictions or sentences after direct appeal: the motion to vacate, set aside, or correct a sentence under 28 U.S.C. § 2255. This powerful tool allows individuals convicted in federal court to raise claims of constitutional violations, jurisdictional errors, and ineffective assistance of counsel. Section 2255 is often referred to as a federal habeas corpus petition, though it is distinct in its application and scope.

8.1 Overview of 28 U.S.C. § 2255

Under 28 U.S.C. § 2255, a federal prisoner can challenge the legality of their detention by filing a motion in the court where they were sentenced. This motion serves as a collateral attack on the conviction or sentence, meaning it is filed after the direct appeal process has been exhausted.

The key issues that can be raised under § 2255 include:

- Constitutional Violations: Claims that the defendant's constitutional rights were violated, such as the right to due process or the right to effective assistance of counsel.
- Jurisdictional Errors: Claims that the trial court lacked jurisdiction to convict or sentence the defendant.
- Ineffective Assistance of Counsel: Claims that defense counsel's performance was so deficient that it deprived the defendant of a fair trial or sentencing.
- Excessive or Unlawful Sentences: Claims that the sentence imposed was unlawful, either because it exceeded the statutory maximum or because it was based on improper factors.

8.2 Differences Between § 2255 and Habeas Corpus Petitions Under § 2241

Though often compared to habeas corpus petitions under 28 U.S.C. § 2241, motions under § 2255 are distinct and apply only to federal prisoners. The key differences are:

- Location of Filing: A § 2255 motion must be filed in the

federal district court where the prisoner was sentenced, while a § 2241 habeas corpus petition is typically filed in the jurisdiction where the prisoner is incarcerated.
- Scope of Claims: A § 2255 motion is generally used to challenge the legality of the conviction or sentence itself, whereas a § 2241 petition is used to challenge the conditions of confinement or issues such as the calculation of good-time credits.
- Successive Petitions: Prisoners can only file one § 2255 motion unless they receive permission from a federal appellate court to file a second or successive petition based on newly discovered evidence or a new rule of constitutional law.

8.3 Grounds for Filing a § 2255 Motion

To successfully challenge a conviction or sentence under § 2255, the petitioner must establish one or more of the following:

1. Violation of Constitutional Rights: This is the most common basis for a § 2255 motion. Examples include claims that the defendant's rights were violated under the Fourth Amendment (illegal search and seizure), Fifth Amendment (self-incrimination), Sixth Amendment (right to counsel or a fair trial), or Eighth Amendment (cruel and unusual punishment).
2. Ineffective Assistance of Counsel: A significant number of § 2255 motions allege that defense counsel's performance was constitutionally deficient under the Strickland standard. The petitioner must demonstrate that counsel's performance fell below an objective standard of reasonableness and that this deficiency prejudiced the outcome of the trial or sentencing.
3. Jurisdictional Errors: If the court that convicted or sentenced the defendant lacked jurisdiction, this can be

grounds for relief. This is rare in federal cases but can occur if the court violated statutory jurisdictional limits.

4. Unlawful Sentence: Defendants can challenge their sentences under § 2255 if the sentence imposed exceeded the statutory maximum, if it was based on erroneous guidelines calculations, or if the sentencing judge relied on improper factors.

5. Newly Discovered Evidence or Legal Precedents: If new evidence comes to light that could exonerate the defendant, or if there has been a significant change in the law that retroactively applies to the defendant's case, a § 2255 motion may be warranted.

8.4 Time Limits and Procedural Requirements

Federal law imposes strict time limits on filing a § 2255 motion. Under the Antiterrorism and Effective Death Penalty Act (AEDPA), prisoners must file their § 2255 motion within one year of the latest of the following:

- The date on which the conviction became final (usually after the conclusion of the direct appeal process).
- The date on which a new, retroactive constitutional right was recognized by the U.S. Supreme Court.
- The date on which the facts supporting the claim could have been discovered through the exercise of due diligence.
- The date on which the impediment to filing created by governmental action was removed, if the government prevented the filing.

If the motion is filed after this one-year deadline, the court may dismiss it as untimely unless the petitioner can demonstrate that the statute of limitations should be equitably tolled due to extraordinary circumstances.

8.5 Filing a § 2255 Motion

The process for filing a § 2255 motion involves several key steps:

1. Drafting the Motion: The petitioner (or their attorney) must draft a written motion outlining the grounds for relief. This motion should include specific facts and legal arguments showing how the conviction or sentence violated the petitioner's constitutional rights or federal law.
2. Filing the Motion: The motion must be filed in the federal district court that imposed the original sentence. There is no filing fee for § 2255 motions.
3. Supporting Documents: The petitioner may submit affidavits, expert reports, or other supporting documents to bolster their claims. For example, if the claim is based on ineffective assistance of counsel, the petitioner might include an affidavit detailing the specific ways in which counsel's performance was deficient.
4. Government's Response: After the motion is filed, the government will typically be given an opportunity to respond. The government's response will argue why the court should deny the motion, often by asserting that the claims are without merit or that any errors were harmless.
5. Evidentiary Hearing (if necessary): In some cases, the court may order an evidentiary hearing to evaluate disputed facts or new evidence. This is more likely if the motion raises claims of ineffective assistance of counsel or newly discovered evidence.
6. Court's Decision: The court will issue a ruling based on the motion, the response, and any evidence presented at a hearing. If the court grants the § 2255 motion, it may vacate the conviction, order a new trial, or modify the sentence.

8.6 Successive § 2255 Motions

Prisoners are generally limited to one § 2255 motion. However, in rare cases, a second or successive § 2255 motion may be filed if the prisoner obtains permission from the U.S. Court of Appeals. Permission is typically granted only in two situations:

1. New Evidence: The prisoner can present newly discovered evidence that would clearly establish innocence.
2. New Legal Rule: The U.S. Supreme Court has issued a new rule of constitutional law that applies retroactively to cases on collateral review.

The appellate court must authorize the filing of a successive petition, and this standard is difficult to meet, making successive § 2255 motions rare.

8.7 Case Law on 28 U.S.C. § 2255

Several important court decisions have shaped the application of § 2255 motions. These cases illustrate the types of claims that are commonly raised and the challenges prisoners face when seeking relief.

- Hill v. United States (1962): This case established that a § 2255 motion could be used to challenge a sentence based on violations of constitutional rights, such as ineffective assistance of counsel or violations of due process.
- Massaro v. United States (2003): The Supreme Court held that ineffective assistance of counsel claims may be raised for the first time in a § 2255 motion, even if they were not raised on direct appeal. This decision has had a significant impact on post-conviction relief, as many claims of ineffective counsel arise only after the conclusion of the trial.
- United States v. Addonizio (1979): The Court ruled that a change in law or policy after sentencing does not automatically entitle a prisoner to relief under § 2255 unless

the change affects the legality of the conviction or sentence itself.

8.8 Case Study: Using § 2255 for Relief

One notable example of the use of a § 2255 motion is the case of Chaidez v. United States (2013). Roselva Chaidez was convicted of mail fraud and later filed a § 2255 motion, claiming ineffective assistance of counsel because her attorney failed to inform her of the immigration consequences of her conviction. While the U.S. Supreme Court ultimately ruled against Chaidez, this case highlighted the importance of raising claims of ineffective assistance through post-conviction relief.

Chapter 9: State Post-Conviction Remedies

In addition to federal post-conviction remedies, individuals convicted in state courts have access to a variety of state-level post-conviction procedures. These remedies differ by state but generally provide an avenue for defendants to challenge their conviction or sentence after the appeal process has been exhausted. While the procedures vary, most states offer mechanisms similar to federal habeas corpus petitions, allowing prisoners to raise constitutional claims, newly discovered evidence, and other significant legal issues.

9.1 Overview of State Post-Conviction Relief

Post-conviction relief in state courts provides a way for convicted individuals to challenge the legality of their conviction or sentence, raise claims of ineffective assistance of counsel, and present newly discovered evidence. These petitions are typically filed in the trial court where the original conviction took place.

State post-conviction remedies are distinct from direct appeals, focusing instead on issues that were not or could not have been raised during the trial or on appeal. Common claims include violations of constitutional rights, newly discovered evidence, ineffective assistance of counsel, and prosecutorial misconduct.

9.2 Common Types of State Post-Conviction Relief

Though the names and specific procedures vary, most states offer similar forms of post-conviction relief. Here are the most common types:

- State Habeas Corpus Petitions: Many states allow prisoners to file a habeas corpus petition in state court to challenge their conviction or sentence. These petitions raise claims that the defendant's constitutional rights were violated, often focusing on issues like ineffective assistance of counsel, unlawful confinement, or newly discovered evidence.
- Motions for a New Trial: In some states, defendants can file a motion for a new trial based on newly discovered evidence or claims that the trial was fundamentally unfair. These motions typically have strict time limits and require the petitioner to show that the new evidence would likely have changed the outcome of the trial.
- Post-Conviction Relief Petitions (PCRs): Many states have specific post-conviction relief statutes or rules (sometimes referred to as "PCRs"). These allow defendants to raise a wide range of claims, from constitutional violations to jurisdictional errors. Some states allow multiple PCR petitions, while others restrict successive petitions except in rare circumstances.

9.3 Differences Between State and Federal Post-Conviction Remedies

State and federal post-conviction remedies share many similarities, but there are important distinctions between the two systems. The primary differences involve where the petitions are filed and the scope of issues that can be raised.

- Jurisdiction: State post-conviction petitions are filed in state courts, typically in the same court that handled the trial or sentencing. Federal habeas corpus petitions, by contrast, are filed in federal courts and can only be pursued after state remedies have been exhausted.
- Legal Standards: While federal habeas corpus petitions are governed by federal law, state post-conviction petitions are governed by state statutes or court rules. As a result, the standards for raising certain claims—such as ineffective assistance of counsel—can vary between states.
- Time Limits: Many states impose strict time limits on when post-conviction petitions can be filed. These time limits are often shorter than those imposed by federal law. Failure to file within the prescribed time can result in the petition being dismissed as untimely, unless the petitioner can demonstrate exceptional circumstances that justify the delay.

9.4 State-Specific Post-Conviction Remedies

Each state has its own post-conviction procedures, often with unique rules and standards. Here are examples of how some states handle post-conviction relief:

- California: California allows prisoners to file a state habeas corpus petition to challenge their conviction. California courts will consider claims of ineffective assistance of counsel, newly discovered evidence, and constitutional violations. There is no statute of limitations for habeas petitions in California, but the petitioner must explain any delay in filing.
- Florida: Florida's primary post-conviction relief

mechanism is the Rule 3.850 motion, which allows defendants to challenge their conviction or sentence based on newly discovered evidence, ineffective assistance of counsel, or violations of constitutional rights. Rule 3.850 motions must be filed within two years of the conviction becoming final, although there are exceptions for new evidence or changes in the law.
- New York: In New York, defendants can file a CPL 440 motion to vacate a conviction based on newly discovered evidence, claims of prosecutorial misconduct, or ineffective assistance of counsel. These motions must be filed in the trial court, and the defendant must show that the issue was not raised on direct appeal or could not have been raised earlier.

9.5 Ineffective Assistance of Counsel in State Post-Conviction Relief

As in federal post-conviction relief, claims of ineffective assistance of counsel are a common ground for state-level relief. The standards for proving ineffective assistance generally follow the two-part test established in Strickland v. Washington:

1. Deficient Performance: The petitioner must show that their attorney's performance fell below an objective standard of reasonableness.
2. Prejudice: The petitioner must also demonstrate that the attorney's errors were so serious that they affected the outcome of the trial or sentencing.

State courts may interpret the Strickland standard slightly differently, but most states follow this basic framework. Defendants may raise ineffective assistance claims based on their trial attorney's performance, their sentencing attorney's performance, or their appellate attorney's performance.

9.6 Newly Discovered Evidence in State Post-Conviction Relief

Newly discovered evidence is another significant ground for state post-conviction relief. To succeed on this claim, the petitioner must typically show that:

- The evidence was not available at the time of the trial.
- The evidence is material and would likely change the outcome of the trial.
- The petitioner acted diligently in discovering and presenting the new evidence.

Some states have strict time limits for presenting newly discovered evidence, while others allow these claims to be raised at any time. For example, Texas has a statute of limitations for most post-conviction claims but makes an exception for claims based on DNA evidence that could exonerate the defendant.

9.7 Procedural Barriers to State Post-Conviction Relief

State post-conviction relief is subject to several procedural barriers that can make it difficult for defendants to obtain relief. These barriers include:

- Exhaustion of Direct Appeals: In most states, defendants must exhaust their direct appeals before filing for post-conviction relief. This means that the defendant must first challenge the conviction through the appeals process before seeking relief based on new claims.
- Statute of Limitations: Many states impose strict deadlines for filing post-conviction petitions, often measured from the date when the conviction becomes final. Petitions filed after the statute of limitations has expired are typically dismissed unless the petitioner can show good cause for the

delay.
- Successive Petitions: Many states limit the number of post-conviction petitions that can be filed. Successive petitions are generally barred unless the petitioner can present new evidence or demonstrate a significant change in the law that applies retroactively to their case.
- Procedural Default: If a petitioner fails to raise an issue during the trial or direct appeal, they may be barred from raising it in a post-conviction petition. This is known as procedural default, and it can be difficult to overcome unless the petitioner can show cause for the failure to raise the issue earlier and actual prejudice resulting from the error.

9.8 Case Law on State Post-Conviction Remedies

Several important cases have helped shape the landscape of state post-conviction relief. These cases illustrate how state courts handle claims based on ineffective assistance of counsel, newly discovered evidence, and constitutional violations.

- Martinez v. Ryan (2012): In this U.S. Supreme Court case, the Court held that in certain circumstances, state prisoners can raise claims of ineffective assistance of trial counsel during post-conviction proceedings even if they failed to raise the issue during their direct appeal. This decision has expanded the scope of state post-conviction relief by allowing prisoners to raise claims that were previously procedurally barred.
- Ex parte Young (Texas): In this case, the Texas Court of Criminal Appeals granted post-conviction relief to a prisoner who presented newly discovered evidence showing that his confession had been coerced by police. The court found that the new evidence, combined with evidence of police misconduct, was sufficient to overturn the conviction.

9.9 Case Study: Successful State Post-Conviction Relief

One notable example of successful state post-conviction relief is the case of Lamonte McIntyre in Kansas. McIntyre was wrongfully convicted of a double murder in 1994 based on faulty eyewitness testimony and police misconduct. After spending 23 years in prison, McIntyre's attorneys filed a state post-conviction petition based on newly discovered evidence that revealed police corruption and exonerating witness testimony. The court vacated McIntyre's conviction in 2017, and he was released from prison.

Chapter 10: Innocence Projects and Legal Aid for Post-Conviction Relief

Innocence projects and legal aid organizations play a critical role in helping wrongfully convicted individuals seek justice. These organizations provide the expertise, resources, and legal representation necessary for individuals to challenge their convictions, often after all other avenues have been exhausted. They are particularly focused on cases involving wrongful convictions, new evidence, and issues related to the reliability of forensic science or witness testimony.

10.1 The Role of Innocence Projects

Innocence projects are non-profit organizations dedicated to exonerating wrongfully convicted individuals and advocating for reforms in the criminal justice system to prevent future injustices. These organizations work on cases where there is strong evidence of innocence, often taking on the most complex and difficult cases where legal representation is scarce or inadequate.

Key Functions of Innocence Projects:

- Investigating Cases: Innocence projects conduct in-depth investigations into the circumstances surrounding a conviction, often uncovering new evidence, such as DNA or witness recantations, that was unavailable at the time of trial.
- Legal Representation: Many individuals in post-conviction cases do not have access to legal representation, especially those serving long sentences. Innocence projects provide pro bono legal services to help these individuals file post-conviction petitions, habeas corpus petitions, or requests for new trials.
- Advocacy and Reform: In addition to representing wrongfully convicted individuals, innocence projects advocate for criminal justice reforms to address systemic issues, such as inadequate forensic science, prosecutorial misconduct, and wrongful use of eyewitness testimony.

10.2 How Innocence Projects Work

Most innocence projects follow a structured process for evaluating cases and determining which cases to accept for further investigation and legal action. Due to limited resources, these organizations carefully select cases where they believe there is a strong likelihood of proving innocence.

Case Evaluation Process:

1. Application Review: Innocence projects receive hundreds of applications from inmates seeking help. They review these applications to determine whether the case fits their criteria. The focus is typically on cases where new evidence (such as DNA testing) has the potential to exonerate the inmate.
2. Case Investigation: If a case is accepted, the innocence project team will begin an extensive investigation. This may involve locating and interviewing witnesses, reviewing trial transcripts and police reports, and conducting

forensic tests, such as DNA analysis, that were not available or properly conducted during the original trial.

3. Filing for Post-Conviction Relief: Once new evidence is discovered, the innocence project will work with the individual's legal team to file post-conviction motions or habeas corpus petitions. These legal filings argue that the new evidence, if presented at trial, would likely have led to a different outcome.

4. Exoneration or Relief: If the court agrees with the evidence presented, it may vacate the conviction, order a new trial, or, in rare cases, immediately release the individual from prison. The process can take years, but the outcome may result in the exoneration of an innocent person.

10.3 DNA Testing and the Role of Forensic Science

One of the most significant tools used by innocence projects is DNA testing. DNA evidence has been instrumental in exonerating hundreds of wrongfully convicted individuals in the United States. Advances in forensic science have allowed for more precise testing of biological evidence, leading to the overturning of convictions based on faulty or incomplete evidence.

Types of Cases Where DNA Testing is Key:

- Sexual Assault and Rape Cases: DNA evidence is often found in sexual assault cases and can be used to either confirm the identity of the perpetrator or exonerate an innocent person. In many cases, DNA testing conducted years after a conviction has proven the innocence of individuals who were wrongfully convicted.
- Homicide Cases: In murder cases, DNA from hair, blood, or other biological materials found at the crime scene can play a crucial role in identifying the true perpetrator or exonerating a wrongfully convicted person.

- Other Violent Crimes: DNA testing can also be used in cases involving robbery, assault, and other violent crimes where biological evidence was collected at the scene.

In addition to DNA testing, innocence projects often rely on advances in other areas of forensic science, such as fingerprint analysis, ballistics, and digital forensics, to challenge wrongful convictions.

10.4 High-Profile Exonerations by Innocence Projects

Over the years, innocence projects have successfully exonerated numerous individuals who were wrongfully convicted. Some of the most high-profile cases have brought attention to the flaws in the criminal justice system and the need for reforms.

Notable Cases:

- The Exoneration of Kirk Bloodsworth (1993): Kirk Bloodsworth was the first person in the United States to be exonerated from death row through DNA testing. Bloodsworth had been convicted of the rape and murder of a nine-year-old girl in Maryland, based on faulty eyewitness testimony. DNA testing conducted after his conviction conclusively proved his innocence, leading to his exoneration and release from prison.
- The Central Park Five (2002): The Central Park Five case involved the wrongful conviction of five teenagers for the assault and rape of a jogger in New York's Central Park in 1989. The Innocence Project, along with other legal teams, helped exonerate the five men after DNA testing and a confession from the actual perpetrator revealed their innocence. The case became a symbol of the dangers of coerced confessions and racial bias in the criminal justice system.

- The Case of Marvin Anderson: Marvin Anderson was wrongfully convicted of rape and served 15 years in prison before being exonerated by DNA evidence in 2001. The Innocence Project uncovered biological evidence that had been overlooked during the original trial. The DNA evidence proved that Anderson was not the perpetrator, leading to his exoneration.

10.5 Legal Aid Organizations and Their Role in Post-Conviction Relief

In addition to innocence projects, legal aid organizations play a crucial role in providing access to justice for individuals seeking post-conviction relief. Legal aid organizations, like the American Civil Liberties Union (ACLU), the Southern Poverty Law Center (SPLC), and local legal aid societies, often represent individuals who cannot afford private attorneys.

How Legal Aid Helps:

- Filing Post-Conviction Petitions: Many individuals in prison cannot afford to hire private attorneys to file post-conviction petitions. Legal aid organizations provide free or low-cost legal representation to help these individuals file habeas corpus petitions, motions for new trials, or clemency applications.
- Investigating Wrongful Convictions: Legal aid attorneys often work in collaboration with innocence projects and other advocates to investigate potential wrongful convictions. They may provide resources for forensic testing, review trial transcripts, or interview witnesses.
- Advocating for Sentencing Reforms: In addition to representing individuals in post-conviction cases, legal aid organizations advocate for changes in sentencing laws that disproportionately affect marginalized communities. This

includes challenging mandatory minimums, advocating for retroactive sentencing reforms, and promoting alternatives to incarceration.

10.6 The Application Process for Innocence Projects and Legal Aid

Not every case is accepted by innocence projects or legal aid organizations, as resources are often limited. Individuals seeking assistance must go through an application process, during which the organization evaluates the merits of the case.

Criteria for Acceptance:

- Credible Evidence of Innocence: Innocence projects typically only take on cases where there is strong evidence suggesting the individual is innocent, such as the possibility of DNA testing or credible witness recantations.
- Exhaustion of Appeals: In most cases, innocence projects and legal aid organizations only accept cases where the individual has exhausted their direct appeals and has no other legal recourse.
- Focus on Serious Convictions: Innocence projects often focus on serious felony convictions, such as murder, sexual assault, and other violent crimes, where the consequences of wrongful conviction are the most severe.

Application Process:

- The individual or their family submits an application to the innocence project or legal aid organization, providing details about the case, including trial transcripts, police reports, and any new evidence that has come to light.
- The organization reviews the application to determine whether the case fits its criteria. If accepted, the case moves

forward for further investigation.
- If the organization decides not to accept the case, the individual may seek assistance from another legal aid organization or pursue post-conviction relief on their own.

10.7 Challenges Faced by Innocence Projects and Legal Aid Organizations

While innocence projects and legal aid organizations have helped exonerate hundreds of wrongfully convicted individuals, they face significant challenges. These include:

- Limited Resources: Innocence projects and legal aid organizations operate on limited budgets, and the demand for their services far exceeds their capacity. As a result, many deserving cases are turned away.
- Procedural Barriers: Post-conviction cases often face procedural hurdles, such as strict time limits and procedural default rules, which make it difficult to raise new claims after the direct appeal process has been completed.
- Resistance from Prosecutors: Prosecutors may resist efforts to reopen old cases, even when there is new evidence of innocence. In some cases, prosecutors have fought against DNA testing or refused to turn over evidence that could exonerate the defendant.

10.8 Case Study: The Work of the Innocence Project

The Innocence Project, founded in 1992 by attorneys Barry Scheck and Peter Neufeld, has been at the forefront of the movement to exonerate wrongfully convicted individuals through DNA testing. Since its founding, the Innocence Project has helped exonerate more than 300 individuals, many of whom were serving life sentences or were on death row.

One of the Innocence Project's most notable cases involved the exoneration of *

One notable case recently exonerated by the Innocence Project is that of Devonia Inman, who was wrongfully convicted in 1998 for the murder of a Taco Bell manager in Georgia. Inman spent 23 years in prison, despite consistently maintaining his innocence. His conviction was largely based on coerced testimony and a flawed investigation, which ignored evidence pointing to another suspect, Hercules Brown. Years later, DNA testing on a ski mask found at the crime scene proved that Brown, not Inman, was responsible for the murder.

Inman's case was fraught with prosecutorial misconduct, including the suppression of exculpatory evidence linking Brown to the crime, and the refusal to allow testimony that could have exonerated him at trial. After years of legal battles, the Georgia Supreme Court finally ruled in Inman's favor, leading to his release

Another notable case is the exoneration of Malcolm Alexander, who spent nearly 38 years in prison for a crime he did not commit. In 1980, Alexander was wrongfully convicted of aggravated rape in Louisiana, based on a faulty eyewitness identification and ineffective legal representation. The victim identified Alexander as her attacker, but her identification was labeled "tentative" by law enforcement, and no forensic evidence linked him to the crime. His attorney, who later was disbarred, failed to present any meaningful defense during the one-day trial.

In 2017, with the help of the Innocence Project and the Innocence Project New Orleans, DNA testing was conducted on hair evidence collected from the crime scene. The results excluded Alexander as the perpetrator, leading to his exoneration in January 2018. This case highlights the dangers of eyewitness misidentification and inadequate legal defense in wrongful convictions .

Here are the key contact details for the Innocence Project and Innocence Project New Orleans:

Innocence Project (National)

- Address:
Innocence Project
40 Worth Street, Suite 701
New York, NY 10013
- Phone Number: (212) 364-5340
- Email: info@innocenceproject.org
- Website: Innocence Project

Innocence Project New Orleans (IPNO)

- Address:
P.O. Box 792808
New Orleans, LA 70179
- Phone Number: (504) 943-1902
- Email: info@ip-no.org
- Website: Innocence Project New Orleans

Georgia Innocence Project

- Address: 50 Hurt Plaza SE, Suite 350, Atlanta, GA 30303

- Phone: (404) 373-4433
- Email: gip@georgiainnocence.org
- Website: Georgia Innocence Project

Texas Innocence Network

- Address: University of Houston Law Center, 4604 Calhoun Road, Houston, TX 77204
- Phone: (713) 743-7552
- Website: Texas Innocence Network

Innocence Project of Florida

- Address: 1100 East Park Avenue, Tallahassee, FL 32301
- Phone: (850) 561-6767
- Email: info@floridainnocence.org
- Website: Innocence Project of Florida

California Innocence Project

- Address: California Western School of Law, 225 Cedar Street, San Diego, CA 92101
- Phone: (619) 525-1485
- Email: info@californiainnocenceproject.org
- Website: California Innocence Project

Tennessee Innocence Project

- Address: 1501 16th Avenue South, Nashville, TN 37212
- Phone: (615) 255-0331
- Email: info@tninnocence.org
- Website: Tennessee Innocence Project

North Carolina Center on Actual Innocence

- Address: 353 E Six Forks Road, Suite 190, Raleigh, NC 27609
- Phone: (919) 489-3268
- Website: NC Center on Actual Innocence

Midwest Innocence Project (St. Louis Region)

- Address: 3619 Broadway Blvd., Suite 2W, Kansas City, MO 64111
- Phone: (816) 221-2166
- Email: info@themip.org
- Website: Midwest Innocence Project

These organizations can provide assistance in post-conviction cases, helping to investigate potential wrongful convictions and pursue legal remedies like exoneration or reduced sentencing.

Chapter 11: Procedural Bars and Timeliness

In post-conviction relief cases, defendants must navigate several procedural hurdles to have their claims heard. Procedural bars and strict filing deadlines often make it difficult to raise claims after a conviction has become final. These legal barriers are designed to promote finality in criminal cases but can also prevent deserving claims from being heard. Understanding how to overcome these barriers is essential for those seeking post-conviction relief.

11.1 Statutes of Limitations

One of the most significant obstacles in post-conviction litigation is the statute of limitations, which sets a strict deadline for filing post-conviction petitions. The Antiterrorism and Effective Death Penalty Act (AEDPA) imposes a one-year deadline for filing federal habeas corpus petitions after a conviction becomes final. Most states also have time limits for filing post-conviction petitions, which vary depending on the jurisdiction.

Key Time Limits:

- Federal Cases: Under AEDPA, the one-year statute of limitations begins running from the latest of the following events:
- The date on which the judgment of conviction becomes final (typically after direct appeals are exhausted).
- The date on which a new constitutional right, recognized by the U.S. Supreme Court, becomes applicable retroactively to the case.
- The date on which the factual basis for the claim could have been discovered through due diligence.
- State Cases: Each state sets its own statutes of limitations for post-conviction petitions. For example:
- In California, the time limit is generally six months from the final judgment of conviction for filing a state habeas petition.
- Florida imposes a two-year limit under Rule 3.850 motions for most post-conviction claims, although there are exceptions for newly discovered evidence or changes in the law.

If the statute of limitations has passed, the defendant's petition is often dismissed as untimely unless they can demonstrate an exception, such as equitable tolling or actual innocence.

11.2 Equitable Tolling

Equitable tolling is a doctrine that allows courts to extend filing deadlines in extraordinary circumstances. For equitable tolling to apply, the defendant must show:

- They were pursuing their rights diligently.
- An extraordinary circumstance stood in their way and prevented timely filing.

Examples of circumstances that might justify equitable tolling include serious attorney misconduct, mental incompetence, or government interference that prevented the defendant from filing their petition within the deadline.

While equitable tolling is available, it is rarely granted. Courts apply the doctrine sparingly and expect defendants to show that they exercised reasonable diligence in attempting to meet the deadline despite the obstacle.

11.3 Procedural Default

Procedural default occurs when a defendant fails to raise a claim at the appropriate time during the trial or direct appeal. Most jurisdictions have rules requiring that certain issues be raised at trial or on direct appeal. If a defendant does not raise a claim during these phases, they may be barred from raising it later during post-conviction proceedings.

For example:

- If a defendant fails to object to the introduction of evidence during the trial, they may be barred from raising the issue on appeal or in a post-conviction petition.
- If a constitutional claim is not raised during the trial or direct appeal, it may be procedurally defaulted and dismissed unless the defendant can demonstrate cause and prejudice.

11.4 Overcoming Procedural Default

There are limited ways to overcome procedural default and have the court consider the claim despite the failure to raise it earlier. The two most common methods are showing:

- Cause and Prejudice: A defendant can overcome procedural default by showing "cause" for not raising the claim earlier and "prejudice" resulting from the constitutional violation. Cause might include ineffective assistance of counsel, newly discovered evidence, or government interference that prevented the claim from being raised.
- Fundamental Miscarriage of Justice: In rare cases, a court may excuse procedural default if the defendant can demonstrate that a fundamental miscarriage of justice would result from failing to consider the claim. This typically requires showing that the defendant is actually innocent of the crime for which they were convicted.

11.5 Procedural Bars on Successive Petitions

Both state and federal courts impose restrictions on filing successive post-conviction petitions. Successive petitions are generally barred unless the petitioner can present new evidence or demonstrate that a new constitutional rule applies to their case.

- Federal Courts: AEDPA strictly limits the filing of successive federal habeas petitions. Prisoners must obtain authorization from a federal appellate court before filing a second or successive petition, and this is only granted in cases involving newly discovered evidence or a new rule of constitutional law that applies retroactively.
- State Courts: Many states also limit successive petitions. For example, in Georgia, once a post-conviction petition is denied, the defendant generally cannot file a second petition unless new evidence emerges or the law changes.

11.6 Case Law on Procedural Bars

Several important cases have shaped the landscape of procedural default and timeliness in post-conviction litigation:

- Coleman v. Thompson (1991): The U.S. Supreme Court held that federal courts cannot hear claims that are procedurally defaulted in state court unless the petitioner can demonstrate cause and prejudice or show that failing to hear the claim would result in a miscarriage of justice.
- Holland v. Florida (2010): In this case, the U.S. Supreme Court recognized that equitable tolling can apply in post-conviction cases under AEDPA. The Court ruled in favor of a petitioner who missed the filing deadline due to his attorney's egregious misconduct.

Chapter 12: Strategies for Success

Successfully navigating post-conviction relief can be a daunting task, but with the right strategies and preparation, petitioners can significantly improve their chances of success. Post-conviction cases often face numerous procedural barriers, and defendants need to present compelling arguments supported by thorough investigations, new evidence, and strong legal reasoning. This chapter provides an overview of effective strategies for building a solid post-conviction case.

12.1 Thorough Case Investigation

The foundation of a successful post-conviction petition is a comprehensive investigation. Whether the claim is based on newly discovered evidence, ineffective assistance of counsel, or prosecutorial misconduct, a detailed understanding of the trial record and the facts of the case is essential.

Key steps in investigating a case include:

- Reviewing the Trial Record: Carefully review all transcripts, motions, and exhibits from the trial and direct appeal. Identify any errors or overlooked evidence that could form the basis of a post-conviction claim.
- Interviewing Witnesses: Post-conviction investigations often involve re-interviewing key witnesses or locating new witnesses whose testimony was not heard during the trial. Witness recantations or newly discovered testimony can play a significant role in exonerating a defendant.
- Forensic Testing: Advances in forensic science, particularly DNA testing, have been critical in overturning wrongful convictions. Ensure that any biological evidence from the case is tested or retested if forensic techniques have improved since the trial.
- Hiring Experts: Expert testimony can be essential in challenging the validity of forensic evidence or demonstrating ineffective assistance of counsel. For example, experts in ballistics, DNA analysis, or mental health may help prove that errors occurred during the original trial.

12.2 Focus on Constitutional Violations

Courts are particularly attentive to claims of constitutional violations in post-conviction petitions. By focusing on issues like ineffective assistance of counsel, violations of due process, or violations of the defendant's right to a fair trial, petitioners can strengthen their case.

Common constitutional claims include:

- Ineffective Assistance of Counsel: Defendants must show that their attorney's performance was deficient under the Strickland standard and that the deficiency prejudiced the

outcome of the trial. This is a common ground for post-conviction relief, especially if counsel failed to present key evidence or made critical errors during trial or sentencing.
• Brady Violations: Prosecutorial misconduct, such as withholding exculpatory evidence (a violation of Brady v. Maryland), is a common constitutional claim in post-conviction petitions. If new evidence is discovered that the prosecution failed to disclose, it may warrant a new trial.
• Improper Jury Instructions: Claims that the trial judge gave incorrect or misleading instructions to the jury can be powerful grounds for relief, especially if the instructions affected how the jury applied the law.

12.3 Presenting New Evidence

Newly discovered evidence, particularly DNA evidence or other forensic findings, is one of the most compelling reasons for courts to grant post-conviction relief. When filing a petition based on new evidence, it is essential to demonstrate that the evidence could not have been discovered with due diligence during the trial and that it is material to the case.

Effective strategies for presenting new evidence:

• Make It Timely: Courts often impose strict time limits for filing claims based on new evidence. Petitioners should act swiftly after discovering the new evidence to ensure their claim is heard.
• Prove Materiality: The new evidence must be directly relevant to the defendant's guilt or innocence. It must be strong enough to create a reasonable probability that the outcome of the trial would have been different had the evidence been presented.
• Use Advances in Science: As forensic science evolves, new techniques may exonerate individuals who were convicted based on outdated or unreliable forensic methods.

For example, the use of DNA testing to overturn convictions based on faulty eyewitness identification has been instrumental in many exonerations.

12.4 Leveraging Technology and Collaboration

Technology plays an increasingly important role in building successful post-conviction cases. Petitioners and their legal teams should use all available tools to strengthen their claims and improve the efficiency of case investigations.

Technological tools for success:

- Database Research: Legal databases, such as Westlaw or LexisNexis, can be used to research precedents, track changes in case law, and identify new legal strategies that may apply to the post-conviction case.
- Digital Forensics: In some cases, digital forensics—such as retrieving deleted text messages or analyzing cell phone data—can uncover evidence that was not available during the trial.
- Collaboration with Legal Experts: Working with innocence projects, legal aid organizations, or attorneys who specialize in post-conviction relief can provide access to critical resources and expertise. These organizations often have experience navigating complex post-conviction issues and can help guide petitioners through the process.

12.5 Building a Strong Legal Argument

A well-crafted legal argument is critical to the success of any post-conviction petition. Petitioners must clearly and persuasively present their claims, supporting them with legal precedent, evidence, and expert testimony.

Strategies for crafting a persuasive legal argument:

- Focus on Key Issues: Avoid overloading the petition with minor or peripheral claims. Focus on the most significant constitutional violations or new evidence that directly challenges the validity of the conviction or sentence.
- Use Precedent Effectively: Cite relevant case law, particularly Supreme Court rulings, that support the legal argument. Demonstrating how similar claims have been successfully raised in other cases can strengthen the petition.
- Address Procedural Issues Head-On: If there are potential procedural barriers—such as untimeliness or procedural default—address these issues in the petition and provide arguments for why the court should consider the claim despite these barriers (e.g., cause and prejudice, actual innocence).

12.6 Case Studies: Successful Post-Conviction Strategies

Many successful post-conviction cases have followed these strategies to overcome barriers and secure relief. Here are a few examples:

- The Case of Anthony Ray Hinton: Hinton spent 30 years on death row for a crime he did not commit. His legal team successfully argued that his trial attorney had been ineffective for failing to secure competent expert witnesses to challenge ballistics evidence. The U.S. Supreme Court ruled in Hinton's favor, and he was ultimately exonerated.
- The Exoneration of Michael Morton: Morton was wrongfully convicted of murdering his wife in Texas. His legal team discovered that prosecutors had withheld exculpatory evidence (a Brady violation). DNA testing later identified the real killer, and Morton was exonerated after spending nearly 25 years in prison.

Chapter 13: Ethical Considerations in Post-Conviction Representation

Post-conviction representation requires a high degree of ethical responsibility. Attorneys working on these cases face unique challenges, such as managing the complex emotions of clients who have been imprisoned for extended periods, working with limited resources, and balancing the duty to zealously advocate for their clients with the need to maintain professionalism. Understanding and addressing the ethical obligations in post-conviction work is essential for ensuring justice and fairness.

13.1 The Duty of Zealous Advocacy

One of the core ethical responsibilities of any attorney, including those handling post-conviction cases, is the duty of zealous advocacy. Attorneys must advocate vigorously for their clients, using all legal and ethical means to achieve the best possible outcome. In the context of post-conviction representation, this can mean challenging constitutional violations, filing for new forensic testing, or seeking to uncover prosecutorial misconduct.

However, zealous advocacy must always remain within the boundaries of ethical conduct. Lawyers must not make frivolous claims or pursue relief for claims they know to be unsupported by evidence. Balancing aggressive representation with ethical constraints is a constant challenge in post-conviction work, where the stakes are often life or death.

13.2 Informed Consent and Client Communication

Maintaining open and honest communication with clients is essential in post-conviction cases. Many clients may be unfamiliar with the legal process, particularly if they have been incarcerated for a long period. Lawyers have a duty to explain the options available for post-conviction relief, the likelihood of success, and any risks involved.

Informed consent requires attorneys to ensure that their clients understand the legal process and the possible outcomes of their case. This means discussing potential risks, such as the rejection of appeals or the potential for resentencing that could lead to a worse outcome. Post-conviction clients, who may have already experienced serious legal failures, are often emotionally vulnerable, making this aspect of ethical representation even more critical.

13.3 Confidentiality and Its Limits

Attorneys are bound by rules of confidentiality, which require them to keep client communications private unless the client provides consent to disclose information. This confidentiality is especially important in post-conviction cases, where revealing certain facts or strategies prematurely could harm the client's chance of success.

However, there are exceptions to confidentiality, such as when an attorney knows that their client plans to commit a future crime. Navigating these exceptions carefully, particularly in high-stakes post-conviction work, is crucial to maintaining ethical standards while protecting the client's interests.

13.4 Conflicts of Interest

Conflicts of interest can arise in post-conviction cases, especially if the attorney previously represented the client at trial or during direct appeal. In such situations, the attorney may need to challenge their own prior work, such as by raising a claim of ineffective assistance of counsel. Attorneys must recognize when such conflicts arise and either resolve them or withdraw from the case to avoid compromising their ethical obligations.

Another common conflict in post-conviction cases arises when the attorney has relationships with individuals involved in the original prosecution, such as judges, prosecutors, or witnesses. These conflicts can create the appearance of bias and must be disclosed and addressed before representation can proceed.

13.5 Managing Limited Resources

One of the greatest challenges for attorneys working in post-conviction representation is managing limited resources. Many post-conviction cases are handled by legal aid organizations or innocence projects that operate on tight budgets. This can limit the ability of attorneys to hire investigators, forensic experts, or other resources needed to build a strong case.

Despite these limitations, attorneys are ethically bound to provide competent representation. This means finding creative ways to gather evidence, such as collaborating with other organizations or using pro bono experts. Ethical dilemmas arise when attorneys are unable to access the resources necessary to provide effective assistance. In such cases, attorneys may need to withdraw from the case if they cannot provide adequate representation.

13.6 Ethical Issues in Handling New Evidence

Post-conviction cases often involve the discovery of new evidence that could exonerate the client or challenge the fairness of the original trial. Attorneys have a duty to handle such evidence ethically and to disclose it to the court when necessary. In some cases, attorneys may face pressure from clients or other parties to withhold evidence that could weaken their case or harm their chances for relief.

It is critical that attorneys resist such pressures and adhere to their ethical duty to present all relevant evidence, even when it complicates the legal strategy. Suppressing or misrepresenting evidence is not only unethical but could lead to sanctions or criminal charges for the attorney.

13.7 Attorney Well-Being and Vicarious Trauma

Attorneys working in post-conviction relief often deal with clients who have been wrongfully convicted or who are facing life-altering consequences. This work can take an emotional toll on the attorney, leading to vicarious trauma or burnout. Ethical representation requires attorneys to manage their own well-being to ensure that they can continue to advocate effectively for their clients.

Lawyers handling emotionally taxing cases must take steps to protect their mental health, such as seeking support from colleagues, practicing self-care, and recognizing when they may need to step away from a case to maintain their own ethical standards.

13.8 Case Study: Ethical Challenges in the Exoneration of Anthony Ray Hinton

The case of Anthony Ray Hinton, who was exonerated after spending 30 years on death row for crimes he did not commit, highlights many of the ethical challenges in post-conviction work. Hinton's trial attorney was criticized for failing to hire a qualified expert to challenge the forensic evidence presented by the prosecution. His post-conviction attorneys, however, conducted a thorough investigation, identified constitutional violations, and successfully argued that Hinton had received ineffective assistance of counsel.

The case also raised issues of resource allocation, as the defense was unable to secure the necessary forensic experts during the original trial. Hinton's eventual exoneration depended on the ethical diligence of post-conviction attorneys who pursued the case for decades despite procedural barriers and limited resources.

Chapter 14: The Future of Post-Conviction Remedies

As the legal landscape continues to evolve, post-conviction remedies are undergoing significant changes. Advances in forensic science, changes in sentencing laws, and reforms in criminal justice policy are opening new avenues for individuals seeking to overturn wrongful convictions or challenge excessive sentences. The future of post-conviction remedies is shaped by ongoing legal reforms, technological innovations, and shifting attitudes toward fairness and justice in the legal system.

14.1 Advances in Forensic Science

Forensic science continues to be one of the most transformative forces in post-conviction litigation. DNA testing, which has already led to the exoneration of hundreds of wrongfully convicted individuals, is becoming more advanced and accessible. Other areas of forensic science, such as digital forensics, ballistics, and fingerprint analysis, are also improving, providing more reliable evidence in post-conviction cases.

Emerging Forensic Techniques:

- Touch DNA: Advances in DNA testing, such as touch DNA (which can identify DNA from skin cells left behind on surfaces), are expected to play a greater role in exonerating individuals. Touch DNA is especially useful in cases where physical contact is central to the crime but traditional DNA testing methods were unavailable or insufficient.

- Rapid DNA Testing: Technological innovations are also making DNA testing faster and more affordable. Rapid DNA testing machines, which can produce results within hours, may soon become more widely used in criminal justice, enabling post-conviction investigations to move more swiftly.

As these technologies become more sophisticated, courts are likely to see an increase in post-conviction petitions based on new forensic evidence, especially in older cases where the available technology was limited at the time of trial.

14.2 Legislative Reforms and Retroactive Sentencing

In recent years, lawmakers have been increasingly focused on criminal justice reform, particularly in the areas of sentencing and mass incarceration. New laws aimed at reducing excessive sentences and addressing sentencing disparities are creating opportunities for individuals to seek retroactive relief.

Key Legislative Developments:

- The First Step Act (2018): This federal law has already had a significant impact on post-conviction relief. It allows certain individuals who were sentenced under outdated drug laws to seek sentence reductions. The Act also expanded the availability of compassionate release for elderly and terminally ill prisoners. Moving forward, similar reforms are likely to become more common, both at the federal and state levels.
- State-Level Sentencing Reforms: Many states have passed laws that provide for retroactive sentencing

reductions, especially for non-violent drug offenses. States like California and Oklahoma have implemented laws that allow for resentencing based on changes in marijuana laws and other drug-related offenses. These reforms are expected to continue, with a growing emphasis on decarceration and alternatives to incarceration.

14.3 Innocence Commissions and Expanding Access to Relief

In addition to legislative reforms, many states are establishing Innocence Commissions to investigate wrongful convictions and provide a formal mechanism for addressing claims of innocence. These commissions aim to streamline the post-conviction process and provide individuals with a more accessible pathway to relief.

The Role of Innocence Commissions:

- Investigating Claims of Innocence: Innocence Commissions are tasked with investigating claims of wrongful conviction, especially in cases where new evidence has emerged. These commissions can recommend relief, such as exoneration or a new trial, and may help reduce the backlog of post-conviction cases in the courts.
- Providing Resources for Defendants: One of the key functions of Innocence Commissions is to provide resources to individuals who may not have the legal or financial means to pursue post-conviction relief on their own. By working with innocence projects and legal aid organizations, these commissions offer a lifeline to individuals who have been wrongfully convicted.

Several states, including North Carolina and New York, have already established Innocence Commissions, and more states are expected to follow suit in the coming years.

14.4 The Impact of Criminal Justice Reform Movements

The broader movement for criminal justice reform, led by advocacy groups, lawmakers, and public interest organizations, is shaping the future of post-conviction remedies. Efforts to address racial disparities in sentencing, improve public defenders' resources, and reduce wrongful convictions are pushing the justice system toward greater fairness and accountability.

Key Reform Movements:

- **Ending Mandatory Minimum Sentences:** Many reform advocates are pushing to end mandatory minimum sentences, particularly for non-violent offenses. These laws, which require judges to impose lengthy sentences regardless of mitigating circumstances, have been widely criticized for contributing to mass incarceration and disproportionately affecting marginalized communities.
- **Eliminating the Death Penalty:** The movement to abolish the death penalty is gaining momentum, with several states banning capital punishment in recent years. For individuals on death row, these reforms may provide a pathway to resentencing or exoneration, especially in cases where new evidence or legal issues are raised.
- **Public Defender Reform:** Advocates are calling for increased funding and resources for public defenders, who are often overworked and underfunded. Strengthening the public defense system is critical to ensuring that individuals have access to competent legal representation at every stage of the criminal justice process, including post-conviction appeals.

14.5 The Role of Technology in Post-Conviction Investigations

Technology is revolutionizing the way post-conviction investigations are conducted, providing new tools for attorneys and advocates to gather evidence and build compelling cases for relief. From advanced forensic software to the use of artificial intelligence in legal research, these innovations are reshaping the post-conviction landscape.

Technological Tools in Post-Conviction Work:

- Artificial Intelligence (AI) in Legal Research: AI-powered tools, such as legal research platforms, can help attorneys quickly identify relevant case law, analyze patterns in judicial decisions, and streamline the filing of post-conviction petitions.
- Blockchain for Evidence Preservation: Blockchain technology is being explored as a way to securely preserve evidence, ensuring that it remains unaltered and verifiable throughout the legal process. This could be particularly useful in post-conviction cases where the integrity of evidence is often a central issue.
- Data Analytics for Sentencing Disparities: Data analytics are increasingly being used to identify patterns of racial and economic bias in sentencing. These tools can help highlight systemic issues that may lead to post-conviction relief in cases where defendants were unfairly sentenced due to discriminatory practices.

14.6 The International Perspective on Post-Conviction Remedies

While the focus of this book is on the U.S. legal system, it is worth noting that post-conviction remedies are also evolving globally. Many countries are reforming their criminal justice systems, particularly in relation to wrongful convictions, human rights violations, and the use of forensic science in appeals.

International Trends:

- United Kingdom: The UK's Criminal Cases Review Commission (CCRC) has been instrumental in investigating wrongful convictions and providing individuals with a pathway to post-conviction relief. The success of the CCRC has influenced the development of similar commissions in other countries.
- Canada: Canada has also seen a growing focus on post-conviction remedies, particularly in cases involving Indigenous defendants who have been disproportionately affected by wrongful convictions. Legal reforms are being introduced to address systemic issues and improve access to justice.

Chapter 15: Conclusion and Final Thoughts

Post-conviction remedies are a critical component of the justice system, providing a final opportunity for individuals to challenge wrongful convictions, excessive sentences, and constitutional violations. While the post-conviction process can be complex and fraught with procedural barriers, it offers a lifeline to individuals who may have been failed by the trial or appellate processes.

The Role of Persistence in Post-Conviction Relief

The cases of wrongful conviction that have resulted in exonerations—such as those involving DNA evidence, prosecutorial misconduct, or ineffective assistance of counsel—demonstrate the importance of persistence in the pursuit of justice. Many successful post-conviction cases take years or even decades to resolve, with individuals, their legal teams, and advocacy organizations working tirelessly to uncover new evidence or challenge legal errors. Persistence, combined with thorough investigation and legal expertise, is often the key to achieving relief.

The Importance of Legal and Technological Advances

The future of post-conviction remedies will continue to be shaped by advances in forensic science, legislative reforms, and technological innovations. DNA testing has already transformed the landscape of post-conviction relief, leading to hundreds of exonerations. As new technologies emerge, such as rapid DNA testing, AI-powered legal research tools, and blockchain for evidence preservation, the ability to uncover wrongful convictions will improve.

At the same time, criminal justice reform movements are pushing for changes in sentencing laws, the elimination of mandatory minimums, and the creation of Innocence Commissions to investigate claims of innocence. These reforms are critical to addressing the systemic issues that lead to wrongful convictions and ensuring that individuals have access to justice, even after they have exhausted their appeals.

Challenges Ahead

Despite the progress being made, significant challenges remain in the post-conviction arena. Procedural barriers, such as strict filing deadlines, procedural default rules, and the difficulty of obtaining new evidence, often prevent deserving claims from being heard. Additionally, many individuals lack the resources or legal representation needed to navigate the complex post-conviction process.

Legal aid organizations, innocence projects, and advocacy groups will continue to play a vital role in overcoming these challenges by providing pro bono legal services, conducting thorough investigations, and advocating for reforms. These organizations are critical in ensuring that post-conviction remedies remain a viable path to justice for those who have been wrongfully convicted.

Final Thoughts

Post-conviction remedies serve as a vital safeguard in the criminal justice system, ensuring that wrongful convictions and legal errors can be addressed even after a conviction has become final. The road to post-conviction relief is often long and difficult, but for many individuals, it represents the last hope for justice.

As legal reforms, technological advances, and shifts in public attitudes toward criminal justice continue to evolve, the post-conviction landscape will likely become more accessible and more effective at correcting injustices. The future holds promise for individuals seeking relief, but the commitment of legal professionals, advocates, and lawmakers will remain essential in realizing that promise.

A recent landmark case in marijuana law involved the 5th U.S. Circuit Court of Appeals ruling that cannabis users cannot be automatically barred from owning firearms. In September 2024, the court ruled in favor of Paola Connelly, a Texas woman charged with unlawful possession of firearms due to her occasional marijuana use. The court found that prohibiting non-violent, responsible cannabis users from owning firearms violates the Second Amendment. This ruling challenges existing federal laws that disqualify marijuana users from gun ownership, particularly when marijuana use is legal for medicinal or adult use in many states.

The court emphasized that gun restrictions should only apply to individuals actively under the influence or those posing a public safety risk, aligning with historical interpretations of firearm regulations. This case sets a legal precedent that could impact gun ownership rights for cannabis users nationwide, particularly as marijuana laws evolve across the country .

In addition, various marijuana-related bills, such as the STATES 2.0 Act and the MORE Act, have been introduced in Congress to address federal prohibition, legalize interstate commerce of cannabis, and expunge prior convictions, reflecting broader trends toward marijuana law reform .

In May 2024, the Ninth Circuit Court of Appeals made a landmark ruling in United States v. Duarte, significantly impacting firearm rights for convicted felons. The court ruled that nonviolent felons who have completed their sentences retain their Second Amendment right to own and possess firearms. This decision challenges the blanket prohibition on firearm possession under 18 U.S.C. § 922(g)(1), which prevents felons from owning guns, by concluding that such a law is unconstitutional when applied to nonviolent offenders.

The court's ruling relied on the historical framework established by the Supreme Court's 2022 Bruen decision, emphasizing that there is no historical precedent supporting the lifetime disarmament of nonviolent felons. The Ninth Circuit noted that laws from the Founding Era did not impose permanent firearm bans on individuals who had served their time, especially for nonviolent crimes. As a result, the court overturned Steven Duarte's conviction, finding the prohibition disproportionate to his nonviolent past .

This ruling aligns with similar decisions from other circuits, such as the Third Circuit's ruling in Range v. Attorney General, and it could open the door for further challenges to existing federal and state gun control laws concerning nonviolent offenders .

www.ingramcontent.com/pod-product-compliance
Lightning Source LLC
Chambersburg PA
CBHW070204230526
45471CB00002B/807